ISBN 978-1-330-48490-6
PIBN 10068055

This book is a reproduction of an important historical work. Forgotten Books uses
state-of-the-art technology to digitally reconstruct the work, preserving the original format
whilst repairing imperfections present in the aged copy. In rare cases, an imperfection in
the original, such as a blemish or missing page, may be replicated in our edition. We do,
however, repair the vast majority of imperfections successfully; any imperfections that
remain are intentionally left to preserve the state of such historical works.

# Similar Books Are Available from
# www.forgottenbooks.com

PHAIUS NORMAN.

# ORCHIDS

## FOR

## EVERYONE

BY

## CHARLES H. CURTIS, F.R.H.S.

FORMERLY KEEPER OF THE ORCHID COLLECTION
AT THE ROYAL GARDENS, KEW

MCMX

LONDON: J. M. DENT & SONS, Ltd.

NEW YORK: E. P. DUTTON & CO.

# CONTENTS

# CONTENTS

ORCHIDS OF LESSER VALUE—*Continued*

ORCHIDS OF LESSER VALUE—*Continued*

# ILLUSTRATIONS

## COLOURED ILLUSTRATIONS

# ILLUSTRATIONS xi

## BLACK AND WHITE ILLUSTRATIONS

# INTRODUCTION

THE object of the present work is to extend greatly the popularity of Orchids among that ever-increasing class of business people who have a great love for plants and flowers, and find in their study and culture a delightful recreation and an absorbing hobby. The arrangement of the subject matter is unique. No previous attempt has been made to group Orchids according to their value for general cultivation, and it is believed that the system will appeal strongly to those who contemplate the culture of Orchids, as well as to those thousands who have newly fallen under the fascination of these wonderfully beautiful and interesting plants. This arrangement should be the means of saving beginners from much vexation of spirit, and from the disappointment and loss that are sure to follow a bad selection of kinds to start with.

In the first group the best kinds with which to commence Orchid culture are indicated clearly, and in the selection due regard has been paid to beauty, interest, ease of culture, and cost. The best methods of culture are described, and many of those little details that make all the difference between success and comparative failure are pointed out. For those who, after achieving some success, are willing to incur the expense of obtaining and cultivating them, the rarer and more highly-priced Orchids are also described; while Orchid genera of secondary importance, and those that appeal by their quaintness and botanical interest, are included towards the end of the book.

This style of arrangement may not please the Orchid specialist,

924

but as there is an unusually complete Index to the work, the advanced grower will suffer no real inconvenience.

Many of the old ideas associated with Orchids and Orchid culture were, viewed in the light of present knowledge, most extraordinary, and even now there are some excellent folk who find it difficult to believe that an Orchid may be a very beautiful, interesting, and useful plant, and not necessarily a weird something, more reptilian than vegetable, that is ready to ensure its own existence at the expense of some other life. To their minds the plant must be able and willing to do something wonderful in the way of insect destruction, or, at the very least, must be an insidious parasite. Many also believe that an Orchid flower must mimic some bird, beast, insect, or reptile, and unless they can find some fancied likeness to these things, they are not easily convinced that the flower you show them is really an Orchid.

Very slowly does this idea die; indeed, it seems to be so deeply seated in the minds of many well-educated people that they will hardly be persuaded that Anthuriums, Tillandsias, Vriesias, Nepenthes, and some other curious plants are *not* Orchids, while they find it hard to believe CYMBIDIUM EBURNEUM, LYCASTE SKINNERII, DISA GRANDIFLORA, and PHAIUS GRANDIFOLIUS *are* Orchids.

Happily, since glass houses have become so cheap, and modern heating apparatus has so greatly reduced the cost of heating, Orchids have advanced in popular estimation. Moreover, the frequency with which Orchids are displayed at the regular exhibitions in London and Manchester, and at the leading provincial shows in the United Kingdom; in Paris, Ghent, Brussels, and Berlin on the Continent; and in Boston and New York in America, has drawn attention to their wondrous beauty, merit, and interest, their great diversity of form, colour, and habit,

CATTLEYA MENDELII

and also to the ease with which many of them may be cultivated by amateur and professional grower alike.

The brilliant hues of Orchid blooms, the exquisite colour combinations so many of them present, and, above all, the grace and longevity of the flowers have done more than anything else to make Orchids popular. The further fact that many of the most desirable species are not more expensive than the best varieties of hardy florists' flowers has induced hosts of amateurs to try their luck with a few Odontoglossums, Cypripediums, Cœlogynes, Lycastes, or Cymbidiums, and with great success. Friends have found to their surprise that many of these Orchids may be grown in a glass house where the minimum winter temperature is not lower than 40° Fahr., and so they have been interested and the cult still further extended.

The huge importations of many of our most beautiful and popular Orchids that arrived about twenty years or so ago gave a great fillip to the cult simply because the plants could often be purchased as cheaply as bedding plants, and small lots were purchased at auction sales in the same speculative spirit as Dutch bulbs are bought. Millions of plants must have been killed by inattention and over-kindness during the intervening years, but thousands have lived to delight their cultivators, and to prove to those who failed that Orchids do not present insuperable cultural difficulties.

One other matter has served to advance the popularity of Orchids and lead to their greatly extended culture, and it is their tenacity of life. Imported plants emphasise this point, for what besides Orchids could stand the strain imposed upon them by being torn from trees or rocks, laid out in the sun to dry, packed in wooden cases, transported over leagues of tropical country, and shipped thousands of miles overseas, and still retain so much life that they start into vigorous growth under suitable conditions?

With some notable exceptions Orchids are not easily killed if kept in a warm, moist atmosphere.

The florist fully understands the value of Orchid blooms in choice designs. Very often these are cheaper than other flowers because of the long time they remain in good condition when cut and placed in water.

The cost of cultivating Orchids is not greater than the cost of growing the great majority of plants needing glass protection, nor, unless especially rare species or unique and beautiful varieties and hybrids are purchased, is the initial cost of the plants greater.

In addition to providing selections, descriptions, and cultural directions of the highest value, an effort has been made in this work to produce illustrations of outstanding merit, in the hope that these may bring before the public in a more striking and truthful manner than words or paintings, the beauty of form and colour Orchids possess in such a high degree. The coloured illustrations are from photographs in colour taken by Mr T. E. Waltham, of Upper Tulse Hill, London, S.W.; while the half-tone illustrations are reproduced from photographs taken by Mr A. J. Campbell, of 55 and 56 Chancery Lane, London, E.C. The plants and flowers represented are from various sources, but chiefly from the private collections of Lt.-Col. Sir G. L. Holford, K.C.V.O., C.I.E., etc., Westonbirt, Tetbury, Gloucester; Sir Jeremiah Colman, Bt., Gatton Park, Reigate; H. S. Goodson, Esq., Fairlawn, Putney; and R. G. Thwaites, Esq., Christchurch Road, Streatham; and from the famous trade collections of Messrs Charlesworth & Co., Haywards Heath; Messrs Sander & Sons, St Albans, and Bruges; Messrs J. Cypher & Sons, Cheltenham; Messrs Stuart Low & Co., Bush Hill Park, Enfield; Messrs Jas. Veitch & Sons, Chelsea; and Messrs J. & A. Macbean, Cooksbridge.

In more recent times hybrid Orchids have come to the front

DENDROBIUM RUBENS GRANDIFLORUM.

in a wonderful manner, and there is no doubt whatever that home-raised plants are far more easily cultivated than imported ones. Of course, the very finest varieties of many hybrids are quite beyond the circumstances of the vast majority of growers, but year after year there is an improvement in the lower-priced seedlings, simply because the parent plants are being more carefully selected. In all probability, as the years pass and the importation of popular species becomes more difficult, we shall find the finer forms of the latter reproduced from seed at home, and so the " weedy " forms will gradually disappear from cultivation.

# HYBRIDISATION, SEEDS, AND SEEDLINGS

THE history of Orchid hybridisation is a most interesting study, but it is an extremely difficult matter to follow the history in all its details during these later years because of the ever-increasing number of those who make a business or hobby of raising hybrids or cross-breds. Not only in our own land but on the Continent and in America hybridists have been busy. No doubt the discovery of the fact that Orchids could be hybridised gave a great impetus to the improvement of plants, flowers, fruits, and vegetables, and led to the conduct of such improvement along well and carefully considered lines.

About the middle of the last century Dr Harris, of Exeter, became interested in Orchids, and he suggested to Mr J. Dominy, foreman to Messrs J. Veitch & Sons, at Exeter, the possibility of raising Orchids through the medium of artificial cross-fertilisation, and he showed Mr Dominy how the work could be accomplished. Mr Dominy was quick to act upon the advice given, and he made a large number of crosses at Exeter and subsequently at Chelsea. The first hybrid to flower was the result of a cross between *Calanthe Masuca* and *C. furcata*, and this was named C. DOMINII, after the clever raiser. This was in 1856, three years after Dominy began the work of cross-fertilisation, a work he appears to have commenced with Cattleyas. CATTLEYA HYBRIDA was the next artificially raised Orchid to appear, and this flowered in 1859,

ODONTIODA THWA TESII.

and though the parentage was not recorded in those days with the accuracy that now characterises the work of hybridists, it is generally considered that the parents were *C. guttata* and *C. Loddigesii*. Three months later, in November 1859, C. DOMINIANA appeared as the result of a cross between *C. maxima* and *C. intermedia*. CALANTHE VEITCHII, still one of the most useful and popular of autumn flowering Orchids, first flowered in December 1859, its parents being *C. rosea* and *C. vestita*. Under the name of GOODYERA DOMINII the first bi-generic hybrid appeared in June 1861; its parents were *Hæmaria (Goodyera) discolor* and *Dossinia marmorata (Anœctochilus Lowii)*, and so, in accordance with modern usage, the name of the hybrid must now be given as DOSSINIMARIA DOMINII. This hybrid seems to have disappeared from cultivation. The first Lælio-cattleya was L.-C. EXONIENSIS, derived from *Cattleya Mossiæ* and *Lælia crispa*; this flowered in 1863. The first Lælia hybrid was L. PITCHERI, obtained from *L. Perrinii* and *L. crispa*.

In 1867 PHAIUS IRRORATUS flowered and was so named by Reichenbach; its parents were *Phaius grandifolius* and *Calanthe vestita*. The forerunner of the great crowd of hybrid Cypripediums that now serve such a useful purpose in our collections was C. HARRISIANUM, named after the Exeter surgeon who initiated Dominy into the mystery of Orchid cross-fertilisation, and obtained by crossing *C. villosum* with the pollen of *C. barbatum*. This flowered in 1869. During the following year C. DOMINIANA and C. VEXILLARIUM appeared, the latter a cross between *C. Fairrieanum* and *C. barbatum*. But at least one other person was busy in a similar direction, and in 1871 Mr Cross, gardener to Lady Ashburton, Melchet Court, Romsey, flowered CYPRIPEDIUM ASHBURTONIÆ, which he had raised by crossing *C. barbatum* with *C. insigne*; two years later he had a further success in

C. CROSSIANUM, derived from *C. insigne* and *C. venustum*. Mr John Seden now appeared on the scene as the successor to Mr Dominy, and in 1873 his first hybrid, C. SEDENI, was flowered. This resulted from a cross between *C. Schlimii* and *C. longifolium.* DENDROBIUM AINSWORTHII, raised by Dr Ainsworth's collection, at Lower Broughton, appeared in 1874, its parents being *D. aureum* and *D. nobile*, and it is on record that this hybrid flowered eleven years after the seeds were sown.  CHYSIS SEDENII and ZYGOPETALUM SEDENII, both raised at Chelsea by Mr Seden, flowered in 1874. From this time onward hybridists and hybrids increased rapidly. The fine LÆLIO-CATTLEYA DOMINIANA flowered in 1878; the first Continental hybrid, CATTLEYA CULUMMATA, appeared in 1881; the first hybrid Thunia, T. VEITCHIANA, was raised both at Manchester and Chelsea, and flowered in 1885; in 1886 SOPHRO-CATTLEYA BATEMANIANA appeared at Chelsea, and was the first hybrid derived from the handsome little *Sophronitis grandiflora*.  In the latter year an artificially raised PHALÆNOPSIS INTERMEDIA flowered at Chelsea, and proved that *P. Aphrodite* and *P. rosea* were the parents of the wild plant already known.

About this time the late Mr Norman C. Cookson, of Wylam-on-Tyne, and the late Mr Drewett O. Drewett, of Riding-mill on-Tyne, both exhibited hybrid Cypripediums of their own raising, and in later years the former raised numerous beautiful hybrid Phaius, Calanthes and Odontoglossums, being assisted by his able gardener, Mr H. J. Chapman, who still manages the Oakwood collection for Mrs Cookson, a collection in which her son, Mr Clive Cookson, takes a deep and practical interest.  The Messrs Sander brought forward MASDEVALLIA GELENIANA in 1886; ZYGOCOLAX VEITCHII appeared in 1887; EPIDENDRUM O'BRIENIANUM in 1888; MILTONIA BLEUANA in 1889; and the beautiful BRASSO-CATTLEYA VEITCHII in the same year; the writer well remembers the sensa-

LÆLIO-CATTLEYA FASC NATOR.

tion this fine hybrid between *Brassavola Digbyana* and *Cattleya Mossiæ* caused at the Chelsea Nursery when it flowered, and the great interest taken when it was exhibited before the Royal Horticultural Society. CYMBIDIUM VEITCHII also flowered in that memorable year, but for a long time it was called *Cymbidium eburneo-Lowianum*. The first hybrid Odontoglossum was raised on the Continent by M. Leroy, who proved the parentage of ODONTOGLOSSUM WILCKEANUM by raising it from *O. crispum* and *O. luteopurpureum*; it flowered in 1890. A year later an artificially raised O. EXCELLENS flowered at Chelsea, the parents of this elegant Orchid being *O. nobile* (*Pescatorei*) and *O. triumphans*.

It is impossible in the space at command to enumerate all the hybrids that appeared from 1890 onward, but a few deserve mention for the purpose of indicating the progress made. DISA VEITCHII flowered in 1891; VANDA MISS JOAQUIM in 1893; SOBRALIA VEITCHII in 1894; SOPHRO-LÆLIA LÆTA and EPILÆLIA HARDYANA (Sander) in the same year; ODONTOGLOSSUM COOKSONII in 1896; EPI-CATTLEYA MATUTINA in 1897; SPATHOGLOTTIS VEITCHII in the same year; BRASSO-CAT-LÆLIA LAWRENCEI in 1897, the first tri-generic Orchid. M. Chas. Vuylsteke, of Ghent; M. Chas. Maron, of Brunoy; M. A. de Lairesse, of Liege; M. Peeters, of Brussels; Mr De Barri Crawshay, of Sevenoaks; Mr W. Thompson, of Stone; and Messrs Charlesworth & Co., then of Bradford, all now appeared prominently in the ranks of hybridists, and the zeal of the earlier raisers was in no way abated.

ODONTIODA VUYLSTEKEÆ created a sensation at the Temple Show of 1904, and showed the great possibilities of combinations between Odontoglossums and Cochliodas, and in the years that have followed many beautiful Odontiodas have appeared to enrich our Orchid collections. In these recent years Messrs Charlesworth

& Co. have introduced many wonderful hybrids of great value for winter flowering, and LÆLIO-CATTLEYA CHARLESWORTHII may be cited as an example. This firm, and that of Messrs Sander & Sons, are at present very much to the front as hybridists, while in private establishments Lt.-Col. Sir G. L. Holford, K.C.V.O., C.I.E., etc., Westonbirt, Tetbury, and Mr Alexander, his able Orchid grower, have come prominently before the public with Cypripediums of high merit and a grand set of Lælio-cattleyas, many of which are bright yellow, and flower in the dull months of the year, L.-c. GOLDEN BEAUTY and L.-c. GOLDEN ORIOLE being a fine pair from this source. Mr Thwaites, of Streatham, has given considerable attention to Dendrobiums, and Sir Jeremiah Colman, Bart., Gatton Park, Reigate, with his gardeners, Mr Bound and Mr Collier, have also been successful in the same direction. Mr G. F. Moore, Chardwar, Bourton-on-the-Water, and Sir Trevor Lawrence, Bart., Burford Lodge, Dorking, with his Orchid grower, Mr W. H. White, have all added several hybrids, while many others who have entered the ranks as raisers will probably be more prominently before the public in the years to come.

Turning from these interesting historical references to the practical side of the question, it will be worth while to first consider the structure of an Orchid flower. The differences between Orchids and other flowers lie chiefly in the structure of the sexual organs. The outer ring of segments in an Orchid flower is composed of three sepals, then come three petals, but one of these is generally more developed than the rest, being larger, brighter, and somewhat different in shape from the other two, and this is the labellum or lip. Right in the centre of the flower is a stout fleshy process, the column, bearing at its apex the little pollen masses, carefully covered by a protecting cap which, when the pollen is ripe, is easily removed by an intruding insect. The pollen masses

LÆLIO-CATILLYA KING MANOEL.

are connected, and may be in groups of two, four, six, or eight, their number being the chief means by which the different genera are distinguished, apart from outer and more readily visible evidences. The stigmatic surface usually lies a little below the pollen masses and on the under side of the column.

Nature has so arranged matters that an insect is attracted to the flower by the nectar and the colouring of the lip, and when the insect emerges from the flower it pays for the feast by carrying away the pollen masses on its head or back. These adhere tightly by means of their sticky bases, and so are not easily detached, but when the insect reaches the next Orchid flower the pollen masses are brought into contact with the sticky stigmatic surface, to which they adhere, and the insect is relieved of its burden and the flower is pollinated. Presently the pollen masses send down minute tubes into the ovary that lies at the base of the flower and forms a sort of foot stalk for it. Through these tubes the contents of the pollen masses are discharged into the ovary, and there fertilise the ovules, which in turn become seeds. At least that is the general course of things; but, alas, when man takes the place of the insect and transfers the pollen of one species or variety to the stigmatic surface of another the various processes do not always follow. Moreover, there is not seldom a development of the ovary that suggests fertilisation has taken place, but when the seed pod ripens it is found to contain nothing but chaff. If all has gone on satisfactorily the pod develops and the seeds ripen, but the seeds are so minute that very great care has to be taken of them or they will be lost.

Hybrid animals are usually infertile, and so cannot perpetuate their kind, and a few hybrid plants are infertile in some degree. In the case of Orchids it has been found, however, that even where the pollen is not capable of fertilising its own or another flower, the flower producing such pollen may be quite capable of receiving and becoming fertilised by the pollen from another and fertile source. In other words, some hybrids may have the maternal and not the paternal capacity.

The time that elapses between pollination and fertilisation varies in different genera and species, but in most cases the effect of pollination may be seen in a few hours, the chief indication being the quick collapse of the sepals, petals, and lip. The period that elapses between pollination and the ripening of the seeds varies greatly. In the case of Bletias, Calanthes, and allied terrestrial Orchids, only a few weeks seems necessary, but in the case of most epiphytal Orchids, such as Cattleyas, Lælias, Odontoglossums, etc., the period is usually about twelve months, or a little longer. It is a curious fact that the longer the seeds take to ripen the better they are.

After the interesting work of pollination, and a record of the cross is made in a stud-book, against a number corresponding to one on a tiny celluloid label attached to the pollinated flower, there follows a time of more or less patient waiting for the seeds to ripen. If all goes well and good seeds result, the next business is that of sowing the seeds. The methods considered necessary to ensure successful germination when Orchid hybridisation was in its infancy, are not those generally followed to-day by the leading raisers. The practice of sowing the seeds on the surface of the compost in which a plant of the same or kindred species has been recently potted is still followed by some raisers for Cypripediums, Calanthes, Cymbidiums, Zygopetalums, Phaius, and other terrestrial kinds, but is rarely adopted for Odontoglossums, etc.

Cattleyas, Lælias, Brassias, Brassavolas, Epidendrums, Sophronitis, and similar Orchids, are best raised in an ordinary propagating case placed in a house where a warm, moist atmosphere

ODONTOG OSSUM SPECTAB LE.

is at all times maintained.  Here, given the same kind of careful attention that tropical and sub-tropical seeds receive, especially those that are very small, there is no good reason why fertile Orchid seeds should fail to germinate.  In an ordinary stove house, with slips of glass over the seed pots, there is no difficulty in raising Orchids, but a propagating case in the same house gives greater protection, secures a more equable temperature, and serves to maintain a regularly moist atmosphere, and its use is therefore strongly advised.  Under these conditions germination is rapid and the seedlings progress better than under the older method.  A proper seed bed is a matter of importance.  A rough sawn slice from the end of a scaffold pole does not at first sight seem to be a promising bed for the germination of seeds that may presently yield a plant worth hundreds of pounds sterling; it is, nevertheless.  A hole should be bored through the centre of the circular block, and the wood be then trimmed at its circumference to fit the pot to be used.  This done, put the blocks in the rain-water tank to thoroughly soak.  Clean pots must be well crocked and have the drainage covered with sphagnum.  On to this foundation the block of soaked wood is placed, and kept in position by means of chopped sphagnum and silver sand pressed firmly in the half-inch space allowed between the block and the pot.  Thoroughly moisten the whole and place in a warm house for a few hours, where it will become warm but not dry.  The seed bed is now ready to receive the seeds, and these must be sown thinly and regularly over the rough surface of the wood.  Directly after the seeds have been sown, place the properly labelled pot in the propagating case, and lightly shade it.  When more moisture is needed, dip the base of the pot in tepid water, so that the moisture gradually soaks up into the wood block.

This is a good method, but there is another that finds more

favour with the up-to-date hybridist. In this case four-inch pots are selected, cleaned, and crocked one-third of their depth. Pieces of calico or fine canvas, about four inches square, are then cut, and one is laid in the palm of the left hand. With the right hand a good handful of finely chopped sphagnum is placed in the centre of the material and the corners are then drawn together so that the whole forms a firm ball. A few stitches or a piece of fine raffia will serve to keep the ends of the canvas together, and the ball is then placed in the pot, with the smooth surface upward, and some finely chopped sphagnum is pressed between it and the pot. Finely chopped sphagnum is very necessary, because if not finely chopped the moss will soon grow vigorously and prove a source of danger to the tiny seedlings. Soak the whole in rain water, and when surplus water has drained away, and the seed bed is as warm as the atmosphere of the propagating case, sow the seeds thinly on the moist canvas surface, and subsequently treat as advised in the case of the wood-block seed bed. If the seeds are sown in spring or early summer, and all goes well, those raisers who have keen eyesight will be able to see a development in the seeds three or four days after sowing, while with the aid of a pocket lens the promise of successful germination will be even more apparent.

As more Orchid seeds are lost through carelessness in watering than from all other causes, the need for close attention and the utmost care will be obvious. At the risk of some repetition it seems advisable to point out that success in raising Orchids from seeds depends a great deal more upon the treatment followed after the seeds have been sown, than upon any special method of preparing the seed bed. Orchid seeds are extremely light in most cases, so much so that when dry they will float away upon the air if exposed to the slightest breath. This being so, it follows that when they are sown the seeds may be washed from the seed bed if

LÆLIO-CATTLEYA CANHAMIANA ALBA.

water is given in any but the most careful manner. The water used should be soft, and at a temperature one or two degrees higher than that of the propagating case, and when the seed pots are gently lowered into the water the latter must not be allowed to soak upward too fast, or to rise high enough to float the seeds off the block or canvas, or even to move them.

The length of time occupied in germination varies greatly. As already suggested, progress may be detected in three or four days in some cases, while in others the seeds may lie apparently dormant for the greater part of a year. This refers to different kinds of Orchids, but even with seeds from the same pod there may be a considerable difference in the time of germination, some remaining dormant after others have germinated and grown into tiny seedlings just large enough to be transplanted. When germination is an accomplished fact it does not follow that all seedlings progress at the same rate. Some hybrid Cypripedium seedlings advance so slowly that a couple of years may elapse before they can be safely transferred from the seed bed.

An Orchid seedling is a very minute body at first, and is in the form of a tiny green bit of vegetable matter, very different from the tiniest seedling among commoner flowering plants. The little green drop increases in size, and after some little time has elapsed a small leaf appears. Soon after this stage is reached the first root should appear, and its appearance may be taken as a sign that a suitable time for transplanting has arrived. Three, five, or more seedlings may at this stage be placed in one small pot, but amateur raisers should always remember that a seedling Orchid progresses most favourably when given a wee pot to itself and treated as a distinct individual. Questions of time and available space have always to be considered, but, as a general rule, time is eventually saved when each seedling is treated as an individual from the beginning, rather than as one of a little colony growing in a larger pot. When several seedlings occupy the same pot one or two generally progress far more rapidly than the rest, but it would not be in the best interests of the majority if these were removed and given a separate existence before their brethren were sufficiently advanced to receive similar treatment.

For all seedling epiphytal Orchids a finely chopped compost consisting of fibrous peat, broken leaves, and sphagnum, in equal parts, will be found suitable, but sufficient silver sand must be added to ensure porosity. For seedlings of terrestrial Orchids, such as Calanthes, Cypripediums, Phaius, etc., a little loam fibre should be added to the materials already advised. The pots must be perfectly clean and, if new, be thoroughly soaked in water and again dried before use. The need for perfect and ample drainage will be apparent because, while it is essential that the compost is never allowed to dry, it is equally essential that it shall not be sodden or sour. Into the prepared compost the seedlings should be placed firmly, and the work is best performed in a moist, shaded house, so that the seedlings are not exposed to a dry atmosphere when being transferred. A watering with tepid water, given through a fine rose, will complete the operation. Sufficient moisture must always be provided, ample shade, and the warm, moist atmosphere of a stove or intermediate house must be afforded for some time to come, and a sharp watch must be kept on the sphagnum lest it grow strong enough to overtop the little seedlings.

Those who raise Orchids for profit rather than for pleasure know that time saved is also money saved, and so they do all in their power to reduce the period of time that must necessarily elapse between seed sowing and the appearance of the first flower. Formerly, raisers considered it the correct thing to follow Nature as closely as possible in their treatment of seedlings, forgetting that

ODON' OG OSSUM PHŒBE

Nature is cruel, and only looks to the survival of the fittest and the perpetuation of the type, while it is the duty of a raiser to secure the survival of the unlike, the unique, the beautiful, with very little regard to natural fitness, because, under cultivation, the plants so selected will not have to compete with others in the race of life. Remembering that most Orchids have a season of rest, and such season is usually a dry one, raisers followed Nature in this respect when dealing with seedlings as well as with matured plants. The result of this treatment, so far as the seedlings were concerned, was to retard progress materially, and, incidentally, to so weaken them that the time of flowering was long delayed and the difficulties of cultivation were greatly increased. Modern raisers realise the fact that seedling Orchids must be " grown on " steadily from germination to flowering, just as the seedlings of other flowering plants are or ought to be. Between these periods a check of any kind is most undesirable. Fortunately, if the conditions already advised, and as practised by the most successful raisers, are provided it is possible to flower Orchids as quickly after germination as it is to flower seedlings of most kinds of bulbous plants. But this fact has only become generally known during the last few years, and the wider knowledge has given a wonderful impetus to Orchid culture by showing that, speaking broadly, plants raised and brought up in the artificial conditions of our glass houses are far more easily cultivated than imported plants. The exceptions to this general rule are to be found in hybrids derived from parents of widely differing habit, or those from parents that are naturally weak growers.

After the initial stages of growth have passed seedling Orchids must be potted as necessary, and, as they increase in size, the compost may, with advantage, be of a coarser nature than that used previously.

B

The requirements of seedling Orchids may well be met by the provision of two structures. The first, a warm house, in which the Cattleyas, Cypripediums, Epidendrums, Lælias, and other warmth-loving kinds, may be accommodated, should be so fitted with hot-water pipes that a temperature of 70 degrees can be easily maintained during the winter months, without excessive firing. If the structure is a low-roofed one the plants will do very well on a raised staging placed over a lower stage or bench on which ashes or other moisture holding material is liberally laid. The upper staging, on which the plants rest, should be made of durable open woodwork. If the structure has a high roof the stage must be raised considerably, or shelves used for the plants, as it is desirable here, as in the case of other plants, that growth should be sturdy, and not attenuated as it would be if the plants were kept a long way from the roof glass and light.

As rain water is most desirable, indeed almost a necessity, for seedlings, ample provision must be made for collecting it. Another item of great importance is shading, and the need for runners placed on the roof so that when the blind is let down it is held nine inches above the glass, cannot be too strongly emphasised ; this arrangement allows a current of air to pass over the glass surface, and prevents the latter from becoming as hot as it would if the blinds were laid directly upon it. The blinds may be of the usual canvas, or better still, made of narrow wood lathes. Ventilation is another important matter, and abundant provision must be made for it both in the roof and along the sides of the house. Excessive top ventilation is bad for seedling Orchids, especially when coupled with free bottom ventilation, because circulation of air thus created dries up the atmosphere quickly and produces conditions not favourable to growth. Nevertheless, means for ventilation ought to be plentiful, so that when the occasion arises the many

BRASSO-CATTLEYA MARONI.

ventilators may be opened a little instead of a few opened widely.

All these remarks apply to the Odontoglossums and other cool Orchids as well, in every respect except that of temperature. For these the winter temperature for the advancing seedlings should not fall below 5·5 degrees, and there should be an abundance of piping to provide sufficient heat without unduly forcing the fires. When the fires have to be driven hard to maintain the temperature the atmosphere of the house has a stuffy, used-up odour, and it is then bad for the plants.

Not so very many years ago the Orchid traders were entirely dependent upon imported plants for their supplies; but now home raised hybrids are the great feature of the business, and in the near future we shall have home raised seedlings of the finer forms of the species also offered for sale. At home, on the Continent, and in a lesser degree in America, Orchid raising is a large and growing industry, for not only are the connoisseurs steadily increasing in number, but also in every garden where there is a glass house, and where there is a desire to grow Orchids, that desire is being fulfilled now that the culture of the plants is better understood and the discovery has been made that home raised plants are easily grown as compared with imported ones. During the last ten years the sales of imported Orchids have very greatly diminished and the sales of rare and beautiful hybrids have correspondingly increased. Of course, the finest novelties realise high prices, but the rank and file of the hybrids are well within the purse-limits of amateurs, from the skilled artisan class upwards. New Carnations, Fuchsias, Hardy Ferns, Auriculas, Pelargoniums, and Roses are sold at prices for which nice plants of ordinarily good Orchids can be purchased. Popularity has followed the general reduction of prices, but lower prices do not necessarily mean a poor plant of low quality; it means that Orchids are being raised easily and by the hundred thousand in the leading commercial establishments, and in smaller quantities, but with equal ease, in large numbers of private gardens.   For the purpose of emphasising this fact, and through it to still further advance the popularity of Orchids, the present work is chiefly undertaken.

From a scientific point of view Orchid hybrids are extremely interesting.   In no race of plants or animals has the pedigree been more correctly kept than in Orchids.   Not only have closely allied species been crossed, but species of widely different habit and from widely removed localities have been associated in the production of beautiful plants.   Still further, in a number of cases members of different genera have been successfully crossed, and to-day we have Lælio-cattleyas (Lælia x Cattleya), Brasso-cattleyas (Brassavola x Cattleya), Brasso-lælias (Brassavola x Lælia), Brasso-epidendrum (Brassavola x Epidendrum), Dia-lælia (Diacrium x Lælia), Epi-cattleya (Epidendrum x Cattleya), Epi-lælia (Epidendrum x Lælia), Epi-phronitis (Epidendrum x Sophronitis), Odont-ioda (Odonto-glossum x Cochlioda), Odont-onia (Odontoglossum x Miltonia), Phaio-calanthe (Phaius x Calanthe), Phaio-cymbidium (Phaius x Cymbidium), Schombo-cattleya (Schomburgkia x Cattleya), Sophro-cattleya (Sophronitis x Cattleya), Sophro-lælia (Sophronitis x Lælia), Zygo-batemannia (Zygopetalum x Batemannia), Zygo-colax (Zygopetalum x Colax), and Zygonisia (Zygopetalum x Aganisia).   Anœctomaria (Anœctochilus x Hæmaria) and Dossini-maria (Dossinia x Hæmaria) are also recorded, but these do not come prominently before the public.   In addition to all these hybrids, hybrids that were considered impossible a few years ago in most cases, there are others in which three genera are concerned.   These are Brasso-cat-lælia (Brassavola x Cattleya x Lælia), and Sophro-cat-lælia (Sophronitis x Cattleya x Lælia).   In these hybrid genera

LÆLIO-CATTLEYA CANHAMIANA.

(if such a term is allowable) the plants are all secondary hybrids; in the first, they have resulted from the intercrossing of a Brasso-cattleya with a Lælia, or a Brasso-lælia with a Cattleya, or a Brassavola with a Lælio-cattleya; in the second instance, the members have been obtained by crossing a Cattleya with a Sophro-lælia, or a Sophronitis with a Lælio-cattleya.

Before closing this chapter an interesting fact is worthy of notice, although it has been incidentally referred to previously. It is that many Orchids formerly described as species, but considered to be natural hybrids by careful observers, have had their parentage proved beyond all doubt in recent years, because similar plants have been raised from the supposed parents. Mr Seden and Mr de Barri Crawshay have solved a number of these interesting problems. A word of advice to those who propose to enter upon the fascinating business or hobby of raising hybrid Orchids is that they should arm themselves with " The Orchid Stud Book," a monumental work by Messrs R. A. Rolfe and C. C. Hurst. It contains the pedigree of practically every hybrid Orchid raised, and so shows what has been already done, and by deduction also shows what species have not yet been exploited by the hybridist.

# THE MOST USEFUL ORCHIDS

## ADA

AN Orchid that ought to be more popular than it is with amateurs who have quite limited conveniences for the cultivation of those kinds that succeed under cool treatment is ADA AURANTIACA. This species comes from a considerable altitude in the Colombian Andees and may be grown with Odontoglossum crispum. It is a showy Orchid, and during winter or spring it gives arching spikes of brilliant orange-coloured flowers. For its colour alone it thoroughly deserves a place in every collection of cool Orchids. If ADA AURANTIACA opened its flowers a little wider than it does, and carried its spikes on rather longer stems, its popularity would be very great. Perhaps in the near future our hybridists will evolve an Orchid with the improvements suggested, and without any loss of the many good points this plant possesses. Given the same conditions in every way as the cool Odontoglossums there is no difficulty whatever in the management of this useful, interesting, and handsome species.

## AERIDES

These East Indian Orchids have for many years been out of fashion, and it is hardly likely they will be ever grown so largely as in the earlier years of Orchid culture. By far the larger number of species need to be grown in a very warm house, but there are a few which come from a higher elevation than the

22

ÆRIDES SUAVISSIMUM.

majority, and these can be grown successfully in the same house as the Odontoglossums, especially if placed at the warmest end of the house, and there are others that require an intermediate temperature.

The Aerides have erect stems, and fleshy leaves arranged in two rows. Their appearance and their requirements are akin to those of the Vandas, and to the latter genus the reader is referred for further particulars. The method of flowering is distinct, however, and none of the Aerides have flowers as large as most of the Vandas. So closely set upon the spike are the flowers of A. FIELDINGII that the popular name of this species is the Fox Brush Orchid. The lip of each flower has a long, spur-like development that is very characteristic.

The best species for the warmest house are A. CRASSIFOLIUM, which has drooping spikes of fragrant, purple flowers; A. CRISPUM, with white and rose flowers; A. HOULLETIANUM, buff and white, with magenta spots; A. LAWRENCÆ, a rare and expensive plant with large, greenish-yellow, purple marked flowers; A. LOBBII, white, rose and purple; A. ODORATUM, white and magenta; and A. QUINQUIVULNERUM, a fine species, white, with rose-purple and crimson-purple markings.

The best for an intermediate temperature are A. FIELDINGII, a splendid Orchid with long, drooping spikes of white, rose speckled flowers, each with a bright rose lip; and A. AFFINE, deep rose.

The last named species can be grown in a cool house, but is usually a greater success when grown with the Cattleyas but given more shade than these require. A. JAPONICUM is a little plant from Japan, and it has greenish-white flowers, prettily marked with violet-purple. A cool house suits it very well, and similar conditions suffice for the elegant A. VANDARUM, which the writer has grown well with Odontoglossums. This has slender growths, and these, as well as the leaves, are cylindrical. A teak raft or a piece of birch stem will serve admirably to support this plant. Its flowers are large for the genus, pure white, and produced in pairs, the spike always issuing from the stem opposite a leaf.

## ANGRÆCUM

The Angræcums constitute a very large genus of Orchids, and nearly all the cultivated species are found in Tropical Africa or Madagascar. All are interesting, some have quite small flowers, while others, notably A. sesquipedale, have flowers of large size and are noble plants either in or out of bloom. There is a considerable difference in the habit of growth; some species are lowly and are best accommodated in baskets, while others are fairly tall, erect, and have large stout leaves. With the one exception of the Japanese A. falcatum (which is a cool Orchid), Angræcums delight in the heat and atmospheric moisture of the stove or East Indian House. All are evergreen, and at no period of the year do they require to be kept dry or " rested," although, as is the case with most evergreen plants cultivated under glass, they need a smaller direct supply of water during the dull months of the year than at other times. The material in which they are grown should always be kept moist.

Many growers use only sphagnum as a rooting medium, while others use three parts of sphagnum to one part of peat fibre, and this simple mixture is the one now recommended. When the small species are grown in shallow baskets, a good layer of clean crocks should be first placed over the bottom bars and on this a layer of fresh sphagnum. The roots of the plant should then be spread

AERIDES HOULLETIANA.

out as well as possible and more sphagnum added, this being worked among the roots and filled in to the top of the basket. If peat fibre is used it should be mixed with the sphagnum. When pots are used, as is necessary for the stronger growers, the drainage material should occupy two-thirds of their depth, the peat and sphagnum being then worked among and around the roots and the whole finished off with a surfacing of fresh sphagnum.

When re-potting becomes necessary the roots must be carefully detached from the basket or pot by the aid of a sharp knife, and the operation is the more easily performed if the receptacles are soaked in tepid water for an hour or two previously. The roots should be washed quite clean and all decaying or dead parts of root and stem should be removed before the plant is placed in its new pot or basket. All newly potted Orchids need a little extra shading for a few weeks.

The Angræcums have white, greenish-white, or green flowers, and though many of them are chastely beautiful, and the elongated spur of the lip makes them all interesting, it cannot be said that the genus occupies a high position if effectiveness aud usefulness are the points of consideration. An amateur starting to grow Orchids, and with somewhat limited means and accommodation, may very well leave Angræcums out of his consideration; but where there are the means and where a representative collection is the aim, rather than a rigid selection of the most useful and showy genera, then many of the Angræcums should be grown, and it must be stated that there are few nobler plants than a finely flowered specimen of A. SESQUIPEDALE, and few more graceful ones than A. CAUDATUM and A. PELLUCIDUM.

But if we adhere to the most recent nomenclature we lose all these three from the genus Angræcum, for the first named is now MYSTACIDIUM SESQUIPEDALE, and the others are respectively

LISTROSTACHYS CAUDATA and L. PELLUCIDA.   This is confus
ing, but it does not alter the beauty or requirements of the
plants.

The most important of the species now regarded as true
Angræcums are A. ARTICULATUM, a low growing plant with
racemes of small, white flowers; A. BILOBUM, a neat species with
white fragrant flowers; A. CITRATUM, a pretty species that bears
a number of small, creamy-white flowers on drooping spikes; A.
EBURNEUM, a strong grower, from Madagascar, with stout leaves
about eighteen inches long, and spikes of comparatively large
flowers that are green with a white lip; A. ELLISII, about a foot
high, racemes two feet long, and pure white flowers, fragrant, two
inches across, and each with a spur six inches long; A. KIRKII,
white, somewhat like A. BILOBUM, and formerly regarded as a
variety of that species; A. SANDERIANUM, flowers white, numerous,
and carried in drooping spikes; A. SCOTTIANUM, of dwarf habit,
flowers pure white and long spurred.   The last two species are
from the Comoro Islands.

The best of the Listrostachys group are A. CAUDATUM, which
has long spikes of greenish-yellow, white-lipped, long-spurred
flowers; A. CHAILLUANUM, a fine species with drooping spikes of
white flowers; A. PELLUCIDUM, a charming plant that bears long
spikes of small white flowers that have a delicate, frosted appearance; and A. PERTUSUM, with white, yellow-spurred flowers.
The two last named usually flower in the autumn or winter.

By. far the most important of the Mystacidium group is the
noble A. SESQUIPEDALE, a popular Orchid that has big ivory-white
flowers with a spread of from eight to twelve inches, and a spur
from twelve to eighteen inches long.   From one to four flowers
are borne on a spike, but often there are two spikes in flower at
the same time on a well-grown specimen.   There are two varieties,

ANGULOA RUCKERI.

one flowering in the autumn and the other in the late winter. A. LEONIS, also known as *Aëranthus Leonis* and *Angræcum Humblotii*, has white flowers and is a desirable dwarf species.

## ANGULOA

Although they cannot successfully compete with the Odonto-glossums in grace and usefulness, the Anguloas, natives of Colombia, deserve a high position among cultivated Orchids. The large fleshy flowers are carried singly at the apex of a stout flower-stem about a foot high. The pseudo-bulbs are large, often eight or nine inches long, and the broad, plicate, deep green leafage rises to a height of eighteen inches or more. All are cool Orchids and will succeed with the Odontoglossums while in growth and bloom, but when they have finished their growth for the season more light and a greatly reduced water supply are necessary, consequently it may be desirable to move the plants to a warmer house during the resting period. Anguloas need ample drainage and a potting mixture of peat and sphagnum, with a little peat added. Potting should be done when the new growth has advanced a little, and the material be made firm about the roots.

The best Anguloa for general cultivation is A. CLOWESII, a species with bold, fragrant, golden-yellow flowers, in which the lip is white or yellowish. A little more expensive, but not less beautiful, are A. EBURNEA, white, with a pink spotted lip; A. RUCKERI, yellow, crimson spotted and with a crimson lip; A. RUCKERI SANGUINEA, heavily suffused with deep crimson; A. UNIFLORA, white, spotted and shaded with pink; and A. UNI FLORA TURNERI, more freely spotted and suffused with deep pink.

## ARPOPHYLLUM

Formerly a great favourite with exhibitors, because it could be easily grown into a large specimen, ARPOPHYLLUM GIGANTEUM has been dethroned by the more showy Cattleyas and Lælias. It has slender pseudo-bulbs, green, leathery leaves, and foot-long cylindrical spikes of small, rosy-purple flowers. This, as well as the similar, but red-purple A. SPICATUM, requires plenty of light and moisture, and a position with the Cattleyas, or at the coolest end of the Intermediate House. A. GIGANTEUM often used to be found growing with the utmost freedom in a mixed collection of stove plants.

## BRASSAVOLA

One species alone makes this genus famous, and it is the large-flowered B. DIGBYANA, from British Honduras. It is attractive by reason of its big, greenish-white, purple-tinted lip, that often measures four inches or more across. The narrow sepals and petals are pale green. The plant has the habit of a Lælia, will succeed with the Lælias, and was formerly regarded as a member of that genus. The broad margin of the lip is wonderfully and exquisitely fringed, and this beautiful character the species has given to its numerous progeny when hybridised with Lælias and Cattleyas. Of less value is the compact, Mexican B. GLAUCA, which has green sepals and petals, and a pure white lip with pink marks in the throat.

## BRASSIA

The Brassias are easily grown Orchids, and as they have attractive flowers, often brightly coloured, and always of elegant

BRASSO-CATTLEYA MARON Æ.

and rather fantastic appearance, it is difficult to discover why they are not more largely grown.   For grouping and for exhibition purposes they are especially useful, and the individual blooms or spikes are first rate for ball bouquets or other floral decorations where bright flowers are in order.   There are about a score of species, all from Tropical America.   These thrive at the coolest and shady end of a stove, or may be cultivated with the Cattleyas, if shaded.   The usual mixture of peat and sphagnum suits them, and during their period of active growth they require plenty of moisture with a reduced supply at other times.  .All the Brassias have attenuated sepals and petals and so the flowers are "spidery"; the latter are lightly set on the spike, in two rows.

The best kinds for general cultivation are :—B. ANTHEROTES, yellow, marked with purple-brown; B. BRACHIATA, yellowish-green with brown spots; B. CAUDATA, yellow, with brown markings; B. GIREOUDIANA, yellow, marked with bright red-brown; B. KEILIANA, orange-yellow, with brown spots; B. LAWRENCEANA, yellow and brown, and its variety LONGISSIMA of brighter hue and with longer segments; B. MACULATA, yellow, with brown spots, and with a white, purple-spotted lip; and B. VERRUCOSA, yellowish-green, with dark purple spots.   Both B. BRACHIATA and B. VERRUCOSA come from Guatemala and may therefore be grown under cooler conditions than the rest; the writer has grown them well at the warm end of an Odontoglossum House, where the latter has been joined on to a warm structure.

## BRASSOCATLÆLIA

The title given to this hybrid family suggests curious possibilities in nomenclature when, in the near future, the several bigeneric or trigeneric hybrids are themselves intercrossed with each other.   For instance, the successful crossing of a Brassocatlælia with either a Schombocattleya, a Sophrocattleya, or an Epiphronitis seem to be quite within the bounds of possibility, and when they materialise, then, according to precedent, a hybrid title expressing their parentage will have to be manufactured.

The most prominent of the few compound hybrids belonging to this family (they are all rare at present), are B.-C.-L. FOWLERI (*B.-l. Gratrixiæ* x *C. Schroderæ*), B.-C.-L. HIPPOCRATES (*B. Digbyana* x *L.-c. Hippolyta*), B.-C.-L. LAWRENCEI (the natural hybrid *B.-c. Lindleyana* x *L.-c. elegans*), B.-L.-C. ROWENA (*B. Digbyana* x *L.-c. Doris*)—one of the best of the group, B.-L.-C. TRINGIENSIS (*B. Digbyana* x *L.-c. callistoglossa*), and B.-L.-C. WIGANII (*B. Digbyana* x *L.-c. Aphrodite*), a large and beautiful hybrid.

## BRASSO-CATTLEYA

In this hybrid family there are some of the most gorgeous, as well as most exquisitely beautiful Orchids in cultivation.   With rare exceptions they have flowers of large size, like those of Cattleyas, with the additional attraction of a large, shapely, and wondrously fringed lip.   Details of cultivation need not be given, because in practically every instance the treatment found successful for the Cattleya parent is suitable for the hybrid, but with the difference that the hybrids are, as a whole, far more easily grown and managed than the parent species.   The majority are superb, free-flowering plants, and though they are a little expensive at present they are within the consideration of the middle-class amateur who has a love for the Cattleya family.

In the following hybrids the Brassavola parent is always

BRASSO-CATTLEYA CLIFTONI.

B. Digbyana unless otherwise stated, therefore only the Cattleya parent is bracketed after the name of the hybrid in such cases. B.-C. ALEXANDERI (*C. citrina*), B.-C. BARON (*C. Rothschildeana*), B.-C. ENA (*C. Lawrenceana*), B.-C. FOURNIERÆ (*C. labiata*), B.-C. HEATONENSIS (*C. Hardyana*), B.-C. HOLFORDI (*C. Forbesi*), B.-C. HYEÆ (*C. Harrisoniana*), B.-C. LANGLEYENSIS (*C. Schroderæ*), B.-C. LEEMANNIÆ (*C. Dowiana*), B.-C. MARIÆ (*C. Warneri*), B.-C. MARONÆ (*C. Warscewiczii*), B.-C. MARONI (*C. Mendelii*), B.-C. POCAHONTAS (*C. Eldorada*), B.-C. SANDERI (*Brassavola glauca* x *C. Schroderæ*), B.-C. SEDENI (*C. Trianæ*), B.-C. THORNTONI (*C. Gaskelliana*), B.-C. VEITCHII (*C. Mossiæ*), and B.-C WELLESLEYÆ (*C. Lueddemanniana*).

The earliest of these bigeneric hybrids were given names composed of the titles of the parent species, but this style of nomenclature is giving place to the more rational one here followed. For instance, the first artificially raised hybrid of this group was named *Brasso-cattleya Digbyano-Mossiæ*, but B.-C. VEITCHII is a far more reasonable name, especially as the hybrid was raised by the Messrs Veitch. For some time Brassavola Digbyana was regarded as a Lælia, and consequently the hybrids between it and a Cattleya were for a considerable period described as Læliocattleyas.

Varietal forms are now appearing, the variation being caused by the use of a specially fine form of the Cattleya parent; thus, B.-C. EMPRESS OF INDIA is a variety of B.-C. MARONI, and B.-C. PRINCESS VICTORIA and B.-C. QUEEN ALEXANDRA are varieties of the beautiful B.-C. VEITCHII. If hybridists had given us no other Orchid hybrids than the Brasso-cattleyas they would deserve the sincerest thanks of the flower-loving public in general, and of Orchid lovers in particular, for in the whole range of Orchids there are no more gloriously beautiful and effective plants than these.

## BRASSO-LÆLIA

Considerable variation is found in the form as well as in the colouring of the flowers of the hybrids composing this family.    In B.-L. HELEN the flowers are of large size and approximate closely to those of a Brasso–cattleya derived from *B. Digbyana* and a labiate Cattleya, although the sepals and petals lack the breadth of the finer Brasso–cattleyas.    On the other hand there is B.-L. GRATRIXÆ, a beautiful yellowish hybrid that has a prettily fringed lip, is of medium size, and has the general shape of a Lælia.    In the Brasso-lælias the large lipped *Brassavola Digbyana* has not been so closely adhered to as a pollen parent as it has been in the case of the splendid Brasso–cattleyas; but no matter which species is used as a pollen parent it is not likely the Brasso–lælias will ever become so generally attractive or popular as the Brasso–cattleyas.

Here again it must be remembered that the hybrids selected are not at present plentiful in such a degree as to permit of their sale at low prices, but the question of price will adjust itself in a few years owing to the vast number of crosses that have been made and the enormous quantities of Brasso–lælia seedlings there are in Orchid collections.    But it also follows that exceptionally fine varieties of the hybrids will always realise high prices, just as fine forms of a species will.

The best of the Brasso-laelias are B.-L. CLIO (*B. glauca* x *L. cinnabarina*), an orange-shaded flower; B.-L. GRATRIXIÆ (*B. Digbyana* x *L. cinnabarina*), a yellow hybrid that has shown a great deal of variation in size and in depth of colouring; B.-L. HELEN (*B. Digbyana* x *L. tenebrosa*), a large flowered hybrid with a broad, rounded, and fringed lip; B.-L. VEITCHII (*B. Digbyana* x *L. purpurata*), one of the best, with light purple colouring; B.-L. GIPSY (*B.-l. Helen* x *Lælia cinnabrosa*), is a secondary hybrid

LÆLIO-CATTLEYA DOMINIANA.

of great beauty; B.-L. THWAITESII (*B. Digbyana* x *L. grandi-flora*); and B.-L. WESTFIELDIENSIS (*B. glauca* x *L. flava*), a bright hybrid with medium sized flowers.

## CALANTHE

In most gardens of any size, where there is a house kept at stove temperature, it is usual to find a batch of deciduous Calanthes grown for purely decorative purposes. The tall, graceful spikes produced by the *C. vestita* and *C. Veitchii* groups are invaluable where there is need for many flowers during November and December. These Calanthes may be successfully treated in much the same way as deciduous bulbous plants that require a high temperature. They have long, thick pseudo-bulbs of annual growth and duration, and need every possible encouragement when growing freely, while, after they have flowered, a long season of rest is necessary, and during this time a warm light position, such as a shelf in a stove, and an entire absence of water, should be secured for them. A compost of fibrous loam, leaf soil, and old, dried cow-manure in equal proportions, with the addition of silver sand, is suitable in districts far removed from towns and factories; but where there is subdued light, especially during the duller months of the year, Calanthes are not so easily managed, and a fairly light compost, minus the manure, is then advisable.

All the plants need re-potting in the spring, as soon as the new growths are seen pushing from the base of the old pseudo-bulbs. The pots must be well drained, and when potting is finished the surface of the compost should be at least half an inch below the rim of the pot, to allow room for copious supplies of water. At first, and until new roots have advanced freely, water must be given with great care; but when the roots have taken full possession of the compost, water can be scarcely given too freely, provided the weather is warm and the pots well drained. In most cases it will also be advisable to give weak liquid cow manure once a week, but in this particular the prevailing conditions must be taken into account, for in or near towns it is found that feeding with manures has a tendency to make the compost sour and produce an objectionable spotting in the leaves.

As the leaves begin to turn yellow not long after they are fully grown, this must be taken as a sign that much less water is needed, but as the flower spikes extend sufficient moisture must be provided to enable them to develop fully. The drier and slightly cooler conditions of the intermediate house are desirable as soon as the flowers expand, for the purpose of lengthening the beauty and life òf the blooms. Quite frequently Calanthes are grown closely together very near the roof glass, and in such a position they are liable to damage during sudden bursts of strong sunshine; careful shading, the moderate ventilation of an ordinary plant stove, and sufficient room for each plant to develop its bold leaves, are points of culture needing attention.

The evergreen species take up a lot of room and consequently are not very popular. They need a similar compost to that already advised for the deciduous species, but the dry, resting conditions suitable for the latter would prove fatal to the evergreen kinds.

### Best Species

C. Masuca is a useful, free flowering species from North-west India; it is evergreen and produces its flowers on two-feet high spikes in the summer. The flowers are of fair size, rich violet blue, with a purple lip.

C. Regnieri is from Cochin China, and is a desirable

deciduous species as it flowers late in the season, after the members of the *C. vestita* and *C. Veitchii* sections. The flowers are white, with a bright rosy-pink lip that is very distinct and attractive; they are carried on tall graceful spikes. The variety C R. WILLIAMSII, formerly regarded as a distinct species, is even more striking than the type, as the sepals and petals are white, shaded with pink, and the lip is deep rosy crimson; it is a fine plant.

C. TURNERI hails from Burmah, and, like C. REGNIERII, is late in flowering, and therefore of great value in Orchid collections. It is deciduous and has its flowers set more closely on the spike than are those of *C. vestita*. Their colour is pure white with a deep rose blotch or eye at the base of the lip. In the variety C. T. NIVALIS the flowers are wholly white.

C. VERATRIFOLIA is a fine old evergreen species that has a wide distribution in India, Ceylon, and Australia. It has broad leaves that are sometimes nearly two feet in length, while its erect spikes of white flowers are from two feet to three feet high. Instead of the flowers being borne in more or less arching spikes, they are in a dense cluster, six or eight inches long, at the head of the stiff spike. This species blooms in late spring or summer.

C. VESTITA, an Indian species, is very popular and useful, and is represented in most gardens of any size by one or more of its fine varieties. The flowers appear in late Autumn or Winter, are large for the genus, creamy white with a rosy base to the lip, and carried in elegant fashion on a long graceful spike. C. v. LUTEO-OCULATA has a yellow base to the lip, and the very fine C. v. RUBRO-OCULATA has a brilliant red base. The variety C. v. OCULATA GIGANTEA has the largest flowers and these are creamy white, with a white lip and a rich red eye. This variety has the additional merit of flowering much later than its near relatives.

## Best Hybrids

C. ATRORUBENS (*C. Darblayana var. Wm. Murray* x *C. Oakwood Ruby*) is a rich crimson-flowered hybrid; C. BELLA (*C. Turneri* x *C. Veitchii*) is a beautiful hybrid, and the pure white, large-flowered C. B. HARRISII is one of the finest Calanthes grown ; C. DARBLAYANA (*C. Regnieri* x *C. vestita*) is best known by its fine varietal forms raised by Mr Cookson, and named C. D. BRYAN and C. D. WM. MURRAY; *C. gigas* (*C. grandiflora* x *C. Regnieri*) is a vigorous and handsome hybrid, more generally known as C. BARON SCHRODER; C. RUBY (or *C. Oakwood Ruby*) is the result of selection from a series of seedlings from a cross between *C. Sedenii Oakwood var.* and *C. vestita rubro-oculata*; C. SIBYL is a selection from the same cross; C. SEDENII (*C. Veitchii* x *C. vestita*) has been raised many times since Seden raised it about 1878; C. S. COOKSONI is a good form; C. SPLENDENS (*C. Darblayana var. Bryan* x *C. rosea*); C. VEITCHII (*C. rosea* x *C. vestita*) is a most popular Orchid for late Autumn and Winter flowering, although it first flowered as long ago as 1859; there is also a pure white variety of this rosy-flowered hybrid; C. VICTORIA-REGINA (*C. rosea* x *C. Veitchii*); and C. CHAPMANII (*C. Ruby* x *C. Veitchii*), a new deeply-coloured hybrid.

## Other Species and Hybrids

Other interesting species are C. ROSEA, a small rosy-flowered plant; and C. VERSICOLOR. C. DOMINII, the first hybrid Orchid to be raised artificially, is the result of crossing *C. furcata* with *C. Masuca*; and C. WINNII (*C. Regnieri* x *C. Veitchii*) is an extremely variable hybrid raised in 1889.

CALANTHE VE TCHII AND TS WH TE   AR ETY.

## CATTLEYA

The genus Cattleya is a fairly large one and its members are found only in America. The name commemorates Mr William Cattley, of Barnet, who, early in the nineteenth century, had a splendid collection of rare plants and was one of the first amateurs to take up the cultivation of Orchids. So keen a collector and cultivator was he that it is on record he possessed the finest known collection of these plants. The collection passed, on his death, into the hands of Mr Knight, and most horticulturalists know that Messrs Knight & Perry were the predecessors of the present firm of Messrs James Veitch & Sons, of Chelsea.

Cattleyas come from the American Tropics, and range from almost as far North as the City of Mexico, to as far South as the Brazilian Province of Rio Grande. *Cattleya citrina* appears to mark the Northern limit of the genus, and *C. Loddigesii* the Southern limit. Many of the species are found at a considerable elevation and are subject to distinct wet and dry seasons, but the great majority may be cultivated in the same house all the year round, notwithstanding the enormous country over which the genus is distributed. There are a few exceptions to the general rule and these will be noted in due course.

The Cattleyas are gorgeous and beautiful Orchids, and it is small wonder they have invariably attracted a great deal of attention. Their flowers are of large size, especially in the more popular species, such as *C. labiata*, *C. Mossiæ*, *C. Trianæ*, *C. Dowiana*, and *C. Warscewiczii*, and they are brilliantly coloured. It does not need many Cattleya blooms to make a distinct and rare display in any floral decoration, nor many flowering plants to provide a striking feature in an exhibition group. But, all this notwithstanding, the Cattleyas are responsible for more disappointments in Orchid culture than any other genus. Attracted by their wondrous beauty many amateurs, and also not a few professional gardeners, have purchased imported plants and entered upon their cultivation with light hearts. Though widely different methods of culture may have been followed the plants have usually flowered more or less successfully the first season, but after flowering they have gradually declined in vigour, and probably long before the second flowering season has come round they have died and been consigned to the furnace fire. At the same time, Orchid culture in general has been condemned as waste of time and money. This is unfortunate. Cattleyas are certainly not the Orchids that an amateur should begin with when setting up a modest collection. The vigour and vitality many Orchids have acquired in their native haunts carry them through the trials of importation and their first year under artificial treatment, then the ebb is fast unless the cultural conditions have been such as to relieve the great strain and restore vigour.

A large number of Lælias thrive under conditions found favourable to the majority of Cattleyas, and so do the Brassavolas and the Lælio-cattleyas, therefore the advice given below applies as a general rule to all these Orchids. As a rule the same round of treatment applies to all, but not always at the same period of the year, for the Cattleyas and Lælias flower at different periods of the year and some are growing freely while others are resting or flowering.

Some Orchids, notably the Phaius, Cymbidiums, and many Cypripediums, are often grown with great success in a mixed collection of plants, but very rarely indeed are Cattleyas a success under such conditions. A house should be set apart for Cattleyas and Lælias, or at least a part of a house, if the greatest possible

CATTLEYA WARSCEWICZII.

success is to be obtained and the fullest pleasure derived from their culture.    In the house chosen there should be a sufficiency of hot-water pipes to enable it to be properly heated without the need of severe firing.    A house fitted up as an ordinary plant stove will be suitable if it has a light position, and a span-roofed house is obviously better than a lean-to one.    The temperature should not fall below 60 degrees at night in the Winter, and the day temperature at that season from artificial heat should be about 65 degrees, with a rise of 5 or more degrees during sunshine. These figures should graduate to and from 68 or 70 degrees as a minimum night temperature in the Summer, with 75 to 80 degrees as the usual day temperature for the latter season.    In very brilliant Summer weather the day temperature may rise above these figures, even with ventilation.

Cattleyas may be grown in hanging teak baskets, in pans, or in ordinary flower pots, but whatever the kind of receptacle adopted it must be drained to at least two-thirds of its depth with clean crocks.    A suitable general compost consists of fibrous peat (with the fine particles removed), Osmunda fibre, and chopped sphagnum in equal proportions, with a goodly addition of coarse sand and finely broken crocks to keep the whole porous and sweet.    The rougher parts of the mixture should be laid over the crocks and the rest placed firmly among the roots and about the base of the plant, the crown or rhizomatous part of the plant being set in the centre of the pot, but raised slightly above the level of the pot rim.

The best season for attending to the potting of Cattleyas and Lælias is when new roots appear from the base of the developing or last developed pseudo-bulb, for some root at a rather earlier period of their annual growth than others.    Annual potting is not at all necessary, indeed the whole family dislikes disturbance at the roots, hence the plants should be so fixed in the pots and compost that there is room for two seasons' growth to develop. When potting is done as soon as the new roots are half an inch or so in length, the plants soon take possession of the new material and re-establishment takes place with the least possible risk of check or injury to the plant treated.

Cattleyas need more light than most Orchids, therefore the shading material need not be so dense as that used for Odontoglossums, for instance. Nor is it necessary to maintain such an excessively moist atmosphere for Cattleyas as for East Indian Orchids. If grown in pots Cattleyas and Lælias should be arranged on open staging over a lower staging, on which is an abundance of cinders or other moisture holding material. It will also be desirable in many instances to raise many of the plants still higher, on inverted pots, so as to bring them well up to the light.

Slipshod watering is the bane of Cattleyas. When rooting freely a goodly supply of water is needed, but as active growth ceases for the year, the supply must be correspondingly reduced and very little will be needed from the time the new pseudo-bulb and leaves have fully developed until the flower spikes have made some advance. Most Cattleyas commence new growth, at or soon after the time they flower.

### Best Species

The following are the best for general cultivation, and they are the most useful. Among those not included here, there are some of exquisite beauty, but they do not flower so regularly or so freely or they are not so easily managed.

C. Bowringiana is a foot or more high and has a pair of leathery leaves at the apex of each stem. Its flowers are among the smallest found in the genus, but they are of a rich rosy purple colour, with a maroon-purple blotch near the apex of the white-throated lip.

CATTLEYA MOSSIÆ.

From five to ten flowers are borne in one spike, and October and November is the usual time of flowering.

C. Dowiana is a glorious Orchid, with large, handsome yellow flowers, produced from August to November. The sepals and petals are yellow and the broad lip is velvety crimson-purple, most gorgeously veined and streaked with deep gold. The variety c. d. aurea has more golden markings in the lip.

C. Gaskelliana flowers in late Summer and Autumn. It resembles C. Mossiæ in style of growth, but its fragrant flowers are variable in colour. As a rule, the sepals and petals are white, flushed with rose or pale purple, and the handsome lip is bright violet-purple, with yellow markings in the throat. The flowers are of large size.

C. labiata is the most popular and useful member of the family, and large quantities of plants are annually imported in the spring months. It has pseudo-bulbs six or eight inches high, each surmounted by one bold leathery leaf of about the same length. The large flowers are bright purplish rose, with a yellow-throated, frilled, crimson - purple lip. Late Autumn is the flowering season. There are numerous varieties, as the species shows a large amount of colour variation. The white and nearly white varieties are the most expensive, and they are very lovely ; on the other hand, some of the richly-hued forms are of very great beauty.

C. Lawrenceana is about a foot high, and is best grown in a hanging basket at the warmest end of the house. It carries several medium-sized flowers on a spike and these are deep rose-purple with whitish throat. Spring is its flowering season.

C. Loddigesii may grow as much as two feet high and its stems are slender and not swollen into a distinct pseudo-bulb as in the case of *C. labiata* and its near relatives. It flowers in Summer, carrying several medium-sized flowers on a stout spike. The colour is pale rosy-lilac, with yellow marks on the lip.    A useful and long-lasting Orchid.

C. MENDELII belongs to the group of which *C. labiata* is the type.    It has large and beautiful flowers in early Summer, and these are blush or light rosy-lilac, with broad magenta-purple lip.    The species is variable in the matter of colour, and it also seems to be growing scarcer as a wild plant in Colombia.    April and May is the usual flowering season.

C. MOSSIÆ is another immensely popular labiate Cattleya. It is found chiefly in Venezuela and shows a considerable range of colour.    The large and beautiful flowers have light rose or lilac sepals and petals and a crimson and purple lip, handsomely marked with deep yellow.    Some of the varieties are of deeper colour than the rest, and there is a considerable group of white varieties, though in all these there is some colouring in the lip.    C. M. ARNOLDIANA, C. M. REINECKIANA, and C. M. WAGENERII (or *alba*) are fine forms of this latter group, but even these show some variation among themselves, and the finest varieties are quite costly. The flowering season is May, June, and July.

C. SCHRODERÆ is a lovely Cattleya of the labiate group. It grows very like *C. Trianæ* and has large and deliciously sweet-scented flowers.    The broad sepals and petals are pale soft rose or lilac, and the shapely lip is of deeper hue with an orange-coloured throat.    It is a free flowering, beautiful, and easily grown species, and its blooms appear in the Spring.

C. TRIANÆ, another member of the labiate group, is extremely variable in its colouring, but it is a fine species with large, handsome flowers, produced from January to April or May, and it has a robust constitution.    The sepals and petals are usually deep blush or rosy-lilac and the lip crimson-purple, with an orange-purple throat.    There is a white form (*alba*) and a whole host of

CATTLEYA MOSSIÆ (PALE VARIETY, WITH R CHLY MARKED L P

named varieties showing some difference in colour and form.

C. WARSCEWICZII, also known as *C. gigas*, is a magnificent species, its splendid flowers sometimes measuring nine inches across, and they are usually borne several together, four or five, occasionally seven, in a splendid spike. It is a superb Cattleya and one that flowers from June to November. It is a strong grower and an altogether desirable Orchid. The sepals and petals are soft rosy-mauve and the broad lip is crimson-purple, with yellow throat and markings. C. W. SANDERIANA represents a very robust and free flowering form of this species, and its flowers are of richer colour than the general type. This has been largely imported and it deserves a place in any collection of indoor plants. As the species passes out of flower it will need attention in the matter of potting, and each plant must be dealt with on its own merits, because some flower four or five months later than others.

## BEST HYBRIDS

Most of the hybrid Cattleyas are remarkable for their beauty and freedom of flowering. Many of them are still rather expensive, especially the finest varieties of the hybrids, but they are yearly becoming cheaper and more plentiful. Some of the rarer hybrids are not included here, not because of any lack of beauty, but because in many cases these are represented by but a few plants and are unobtainable at present. The following have proved to be splendid Orchids and, mostly, they are free growers:—
C. FABIA (*C. Dowiana* x *C. labiata*), Autumn flowering; C. FERNANDI (*C. Acklandiæ* x *C. Warscewiczii*), also known as *C. Fernand Denis*; C. FLAVESCENS, a pretty, yellowish hybrid between *C. luteola* and *C. Trianæ*; C. FREDERICKIÆ (*C. Dowiana* x *C. Mossiæ*), also known as *C. Empress Frederick*; C. HARDYANA

(*C. Dowiana* × *C. Warscewiczii*), a grand, late Summer flowering hybrid and one that has occurred naturally as well as artificially and been imported in some quantity; C. HARRISIÆ (*C. Mossiæ* × *C. Schilleriana*; C. IRIS, a fine and useful hybrid between *C. bicolor* and *C. Dowiana*; C. KIENASTIANA (*C. Dowiana* × *C. Lueddemanniana*); C. MANTINII (*C. Bowringiana* × *C. Dowiana*), a very free flowering and useful hybrid; C. MARONI (*C. Dowiana* × *C. velutina*); C. PITTIÆ (*C. Dowiana* × *C. Harrisoniæ*); C. ROTHSCHILDEANA (*C. Dowiana* × *C. Gaskelliana*), a splendid hybrid, also known as *C. Lord Rothschild*; and C. WHITEI (*C. Schilleriana* × *C. Warneri*).

### OTHER SPECIES AND HYBRIDS

Species that are of less general value than those already referred to are C. ACKLANDIÆ, C. CITRINA, yellow, sweetly-scented flowers, grows head downwards and will succeed in the cool house during the warm months of the year; C. FORBESII, C. GRANULOSA, C. GUTTATA, C. INTERMEDIA, C. MAXIMA, C. LUEDDEMANNIANA, C. PERCIVALIANA, C. REX, C. SCHILLERIANA, C. SKINNERII, C. SUPERBA, C. WALKERIANA, and C. WARNERI.

Hybrids that growers should endeavour to see are C. ADONIS (*C. Mossiæ* × *C. Warscewiczii*); C. BROWNIÆ (*C. Bowringiana* × *C. Harrisoniæ*); C. CECILIÆ (*C. Lawrenceana* × *C. Trianæ*); C. CHARLESWORTHII (*C. Bowringiana* × *C. superba*); C. EDWARDI (*C. Schilleriana* × *C. Warscewiczii*); C. FOWLERI (*C. Hardyana* × *C. Leopoldii*); C. FULVESCENS (*C. Dowiana* × *C. Forbesii*); C. GERMANIA (*C. granulosa* × *C. Hardyana*); C. GOOSENSIANA (*C. Gaskelliana* × *C. Schilleriana*); C. LAWRE-MOSSIÆ (*C. Lawrenceana* × *C. Mossiæ*); C. MINUCIA, (*C. Loddigesii* × *C. Warscewiczii*); C. MURRAYI (*C. Lawrenceana* × *C. Mendelii*); C. OCTAVIA (*C. Dowiana* × *C. Mendelii*); C.

CATTLEYA ROBERTII.

OLIVIA (*C. intermedia* x *C. Trianæ*); C. PARTHENIA (*C. Isabella* x *C. Mossiæ*); C. PEETERSIÆ (*C. Gaskelliana* x *C. Warnerii*); C. PORTIA (*C. Bowringiana* x *C. labiata*); C. TRIUMPHANS (*C. Dowiana* x *C. Rex*); C. VICTORIA REGINA (*C. labiata* x *C. Leopoldii*); C. WAVRINIÆ (*C. Loddegesii* x *C. Rex*); C. WEND-LANDIANA (*C. Bowringiana* x *C. Warscewiczii*); C. WHITELEYÆ (*C. Bowringiana* x *C. Hardyana*); and C. WIGANI (*C. Dowiana* x *Schilleriana*).

## CHYSIS

The several species and hybrids of Chysis form a little group that only misses by a very little a position among the most useful and beautiful Orchids. The flowers are from two to three inches across, fleshy, and carried three to eight together in sturdy spikes. Grown in pans or baskets and suspended from the roof in an Intermediate House, the plants are quite easily managed. The compost should consist of twice as much sphagnum as peat, and be placed over ample drainage. The pseudo-bulbs are fusiform and the foliage deciduous. The cultural advice given for Catasetums will apply to this genus, except that when they are at rest the plants should be placed at the cool end of the Cattleya House, or in a similar position as regards temperature and sunlight.

It is a very difficult matter to choose between the several kinds, as all are of equal merit. The beginner will not do wrong, however, in choosing C. AUREA and C. BRACTESCENS to start with. The former has yellow flowers, and the latter white flowers with yellow and white lip. The flowers of C. LAEVIS are yellow and orange, with crimson marks on the lip; while those of C. LIMMINGHII are white and purple, with some yellow on the lip. There are three hybrids, *i.e.* C. CHELSONI (*C. bractescens* x *C. lævis*), raised in 1874; C. LANGLEYENSIS (*C. bractescens* x *C. Chelsoni*), and C. SEDENI (*C. bractescens* x *C. Limminghii*). All are worthy of culture where space permits. A word of caution is necessary against giving any of the Chysis much water just as new growth commences, because the new spikes advance at the same time and an excess of moisture will cause one or both to damp and die. C. AUREA has been successfully grown under slightly cooler conditions than here advised.

## COCHLIODA

One member of this little South American family merits special attention and deserves a place in every collection of cool Orchids. It is C. NOETZLIANA. Treated like a cool Odontoglossum this species produces spikes of orange-scarlet flowers during the Winter or early Spring. These flowers are rounded, closely set on the spike, and resemble small Odontoglossums. The plant is also of great interest, because it has proved of immense value to the hybridists, who have wedded it to various Odonto glossums and thus produced the numerous, beautiful, and growing family of Odontiodas (which see). The other three species are not nearly so valuable. C. ROSEA has small rosy flowers; C. SANGUINEA has reddish flowers; and C. VULCANICA has comparatively large deep rose flowers. A title formerly used for the Cochliodas was Mesospinidium.

## CŒLOGYNE

About fifty species of Cœlogyne are in cultivation, but scarcely a dozen species are found in private collections. The popularity of the genus depends chiefly upon the beauty and usefulness of one species, *i.e. Cælogyne cristata.* It was on this the genus was

CHYS S BRACTESCENS.

founded in 1825, and now that the greater part of a century has elapsed it is still first and foremost in general estimation. The distribution of the plants is through Northern India, Burmah, and the Malaya. From a cultural point of view these Orchids are divisable into two groups, one group needing abundance of heat and moisture and the other succeeding under comparatively cool conditions.

Equal parts of peat and sphagnum make up a suitable potting mixture, but in districts far removed from the smoke of a factory town, some fibrous loam may be added with advantage for those kinds that grow under the cooler treatment. The plants are pseudo-bulbous, and in some cases the pseudo-bulbs are elongated, and in others round or egg-shaped; these are ribbed in some species, notably in *C. corrugata*, and smooth in *C. cristata*.

Cœlogynes are evergreen and therefore must not be severely rested, or allowed to become quite dry when not in active growth. The best time to re-pot, as in the case of most Orchids, is when new roots are being formed, and this is generally a little while after the plants have finished flowering. The temperate species appreciate warmer and rather close conditions for a few weeks after they are potted, as they are then able to re-establish themselves quickly in the new compost.

## BEST SPECIES

C. ASPERATA is a strong grower, its leaves often rising two feet high; the flowers, borne a dozen or so together in drooping racemes, measure three inches across, and are pale yellow, with bright red-brown and orange markings on the lip. It is a free flowering species that should be grown in the stove and wintered in the Cattleya House or Intermediate House.

C. BARBATA hails from Assam and should be grown with

*C. cristata.* The flowers are produced in the Winter, carried erect, have a diameter of from two to three inches, and are pure white with a marginal fringe and crests of deep brown hairs. The whole plant rarely exceeds fifteen inches in height.

C. CORRUGATA comes from the hilly districts of Southern India and is a success under the same conditions as C. cristata. It is a compact plant, about nine inches high, Summer flowering, and bears erect spikes of fairly large flowers. The latter are pure white, with a central yellow, orange-marked area on the lip.

C. CRISTATA is quite frequently grown with a fair amount of success in the same house as Odontoglossums, but is seen at its best when given a slightly warmer position and rather less ventilation. Failing a special position it should be placed at the warmest end of the Cool House for the Summer season, and be moved to the lighter, drier, and warmer conditions usually provided for Cattleyas during the Winter. The pure white flowers, three or four inches across, are borne six or eight together in graceful drooping racemes in Winter or Spring; if allowed to expand in a cool house they soon discolour. In the type the lip is crested with yellow and has a central blotch of the same colour. In the variety C. C. LEMONIANA the colour on the lip is pale lemon yellow, while in C. C. ALBA the blooms are entirely white. The flowers of this very beautiful and chaste Orchid are valuable for many kinds of floral decorations, especially for bouquets, but they must be handled with care because bruised portions turn brown or black quickly. When the spikes are cut they must not be severed close to the pseudo-bulb, for it is from the sheathing base of the spike that the new growth comes, so that close cutting spoils the prospects for the following season.

C. DAYANA is a remarkable Bornean species that flowers in late Spring or early Summer. It is a strong grower and is best managed in a basket or pan suspended from the roof in the hottest

Stove or East Indian House.    Considered individually the blooms are not large or very attractive, the colour being pale ochreous yellow, with chocolate brown lines and blotch on the lighter, often whitish, lip.    But these flowers are borne on graceful pendulous racemes from two to three feet long, and one of these racemes will consist of two dozen blooms.    A good specimen carrying a number of these floral necklaces makes a charming picture.

C. MASSANGEANA comes from Assam and has much the same habit as *C. Dayana*, but is not quite such a strong grower.    Moreover, it will succeed in less heat than is necessary for the latter species.    The Intermediate House will suit it.    The pendulous racemes carry twenty or more flowers, which are light yellow, with a brown lip that is veined and crested with bright yellow and edged with white.

C. OCELLATA, a pretty, compact species about nine inches high, is best grown in a shallow pan, with the Odontoglossums, and wintered with the Cattleyas.    It has semi-erect spikes of white flowers, the lip having two yellow, orange-circled spots and a brown throat.    C. OCELLATA MAXIMA has flowers three inches across, and sweetly scented.

C. PANDURATA is a very striking Orchid, and its large flowers invariably attract attention and comment because of their unusual colouring.    The sepals and petals are green, while the fiddle-shaped, warted lip is yellowish green, heavily veined and blotched with black. The long, semi-drooping spikes carry five or six flowers.    The leaves are from eighteen inches to two feet in length, and the oval, compressed pseudo-bulbs are set rather widely apart on the stout rhizome, consequently a long raft or basket is needed to accommodate the plant.    As this interesting species comes chiefly from the hot, moist parts of Borneo a hot, moist position must be provided for it. The writer has grown it with considerable success in sphagnum and

D

crocks, in a teak raft, suspended over the heated water tank in a hot propagating house.

C. SPECIOSA grows about nine inches high, and carries a pair of flowers on a short, erect spike.  These flowers are nearly four inches across, with narrow, buff-green sepals and petals, and a large yellowish lip that is heavily marked and crested with crimson-brown, and has a white apex.  Should be grown with *C. cristata*.

### OTHER SPECIES

Other interesting and in many cases beautiful species include C. CUMINGII, C. ELATA, C. FULIGINOSA, C. OCHRACEA, C. PELTASTES (a miniature *C. pandurata*), C. SANDERÆ, C. SANDERIANA, C. TOMENTOSA, and C. VEITCHII.  The majority have white, yellow-marked flowers.

## CYMBIDIUM

Although most of the Cymbidiums are large and strong growing plants and are therefore not suitable for small houses, several species and hybrids occupy a foremost position among easily grown and useful Orchids.  A number of the species are of small account, but half a dozen may be selected as thoroughly worthy of cultivation.  All these require plenty of root room, good drainage, and a compost of roughly broken fibrous peat and loam, and sand.  An abundance of water is necessary when new growth or flower spikes are being produced, and even when not in active growth the plants must not lack moisture, though the amount needed to keep them healthy at that period will be relatively small.  Many people grow these Cymbidiums in a Cool House, while it is no uncommon thing to find *Cymbidium Lowianum* growing in a quite warm house with a mixed collection

CATTLEYA SCHRŒDER.Æ.

of plants. A temperature that averages about five degrees higher than that afforded Odontoglossums is admirably suited to the Cymbidiums here described.

## BEST SPECIES

C. EBURNEUM comes from the hills of Northern India and is found at a considerable elevation. The long, narrow, grassy leafage is gracefully curved, and the fairly large flowers are borne in twos or threes on erect spikes. The flowering season is late Winter or Spring, and the fragrant blooms, pure white, with a yellow band and crest on the lip, are very beautiful and serviceable. A large specimen carrying a dozen or more spikes is a fine picture.

C. GIGANTEUM flowers in the Winter, the long spikes carrying from six to fifteen fragrant blooms, that are yellowish green, striped with tawny red, and have a yellow, crimson marked lip. This and *C. grandiflorum* do not flower so freely as *C. Lowianum*.

C. GRANDIFLORUM is often grown under the old and erroneous title of *C. Hookerianum*. It has flowers five inches across, sepals broad, yellowish green, spotted at the base with brown-purple; lip light yellow, spotted and speckled with red and crimson. There are sometimes as many as a dozen flowers on a spike.

C. INSIGNE is a charming species that has lately become very popular by reason of its grace and adaptability to cultivation. It was found in Annam early in 1901, in ravines, at an altitude of from 4000 feet to 5000 feet. The narrow leaves are three feet long, and the erect spikes rise four feet high and upwards, bearing about a dozen flowers (more or less according to the strength of the plant) at the upper portion. Each bloom is three or four inches across, and has white, pink, or rosy sepals and petals, spotted right at the base with red; the lip is broad, three-lobed, usually of the same colour as the sepals, or darker, and freely marked with bright crimson. The species has proved variable in the matter of colour, consequently several varietal names have been given, such as C. I. SANDERI, C. I. SANDERÆ, C. I. SPLENDENS, C. I. SUPERBUM, etc. The erect spike and distinct colouring mark C. INSIGNE as one of the finest species introduced in recent years. The cool end of the Intermediate House provides a suitable temperature for it.

C. LOWIANUM is the most popular member of the genus, and deservedly so, as it is readily cultivated, soon develops into a large specimen, and produces from one dozen to three dozen flowers on its long, graceful, drooping spikes. As an exhibition plant it is held in high favour because the flowers last such a long time in good condition. The individual blooms are four inches across, yellow-green, with faint brown lines, and a lip that is cream coloured, with brighter side lobes and a large horse-shoe shaped blotch at the apex. C. LOWIANUM flowers late in the Winter and continues in perfection for from two to three months, and where several plants are grown the flowers are generally available from February to May.

C. TRACYANUM has large, attractive flowers, five inches across; sepals and petals yellowish green, with interrupted longitudinal lines of crimson; lip yellow, crimson-striped, and with a cream-white, crimson-spotted apex. A splendid Cymbidium, ranking next in importance to *C. Lowianum* and *C. eburneum*.

### BEST HYBRIDS

The best hybrids are C. VEITCHII (the name now given to the hybrids popularly known as *C. eburneo-Lowianum* and *C. Lowio-eburneum*. It is now the custom to give the same name to the progeny of any two species even when the seed parents are different. In the case of C. VEITCHII the original *C. eburneum* x *C. Lowianum* cross has cream-white flowers with a distinct

horse-shoe shaped crimson mark on the apex of the lip, while the reverse cross, *i.e. C. Lowianum* x *C. eburneum*, has white flowers with a crimson mark on the lip, and is the finer plant of the two, and it would therefore seem advisable to give it a varietal name to distinguish it from the original form of the hybrid.

C. WINNIANUM is another fine plant and is the result of crossing *C. giganteum* with *C. Mastersii*. This has fairly large flowers on long spikes and they are white, with a crimson-spotted lip. The finely marked and large flowered C. BENNETT-PÖEI, derived from *C. giganteum* x *C. Tracyanum* is another desirable hybrid.

### OTHER SPECIES AND HYBRIDS

There are several species of Cymbidium quite worthy of cultivation in a large collection, and one of the best of these is C. DEVONIANUM, a broad-leaved plant about eighteen inches high, bearing pendulous racemes of numerous, comparatively small flowers that are green, spotted with crimson, and have a crimson-purple lip. This should be grown in a shallow pan or basket. C. ELEGANS (formerly known as *Cyperorchis elegans*) has narrow leaves, and semi-pendant spikes of light, greenish yellow flowers, that are set closely together and do not expand widely. C. ENSIFOLIUM, a strong grower with yellow-green, purple-marked flowers, and C. TIGRINUM, a low-growing species with green flowers, and a white and purple lip, are both attractive, while C. MASTERSII (also known as *Cyperorchis Mastersii*), which carries from six to ten white flowers on an erect spike, and has the lip spotted with rose-purple, is worthy of attention.

Other hybrids than those already named include C. CHARLESWORTHII (*C. Lowianum* x *C. Mastersii*), C. LOW-GRINUM (*C. Lowianum* × *C. tigrinum*), C. MARONI (*C. grandiflorum* ×

*C. Mastersii*), C. SEDENI (*C. grandiflorum* x *C. Lowianum*), and C. WIGANIANUM (*C. eburneum* x *C. Tracyanum*), all of which are good, but several of them are rare and not in general cultivation.

## CYPRIPEDIUM

A question quite frequently asked is " Which Orchids shall I begin with?" and with very rare exceptions the answer is "The cool Cypripediums." Taken as a family the Cypripediums are very easily cultivated, and even where there are no special facilities for Orchid culture they may be managed successfully if there is a small stove and a warm greenhouse. All the Cypripediums are interesting and curious by reason of the peculiar shape of their flowers; most of them are effective, handsome, and useful, but very few can properly be called pretty. The fact that the greater number of the species, hybrids, and varieties which thrive under comparatively cool conditions also flower during the Winter, gives to this group a high horticultural value, and to this virtue must be added another, viz. the wonderful duration of the flowers, these lasting in fine condition for upwards of four weeks.

The upper part of a Cypripedium flower is called the dorsal sepal; less conspicuous, usually lacking size and colour, and placed behind the lip, is the ventral sepal; the two segments that extend more or less at right angles with the dorsal sepal are the petals; the lip, or labellum, is invariably pouched, but the pouch varies considerably in size and shape; in the centre of the flower, where the lip is attached, is a flattish, shield-like process, usually glistening, and known as the staminode; behind the staminode is the stigma, with two pollen masses near by. In *Cypripedium niveum* and *C. bellatulum* the flowers are rounded,

CYPRIPEDIUM CURTISII.

the sepals and petals being fairly even in size. In *C. caudatum* the petals are abnormally elongated and ribbon-like. In *C. Chamberlainianum* the petals are curiously twisted. In *C. Schlimii* and *C. niveum* the lip is quite small, but in *C. Curtisii, C. Roths childianum*, and *C. Stonei* this organ is greatly enlarged.

Botanists have in recent years divided the large genus of Cypripedium into four groups, and constituted each group a separate genus. From this arrangement it would appear that the hardy and deciduous species, like *C. calceolus* and *C. spectabile*, are true Cypripediums; the species from Tropical Asia, such as *C. insigne, C. Curtisii, C. Lawrenceanum*, etc., are Paphiopedilums. The Tropical American species, such as *C. caudatum, C. grande*, and *C. longifolium* are Phragmopedilums; while a few species (not referred to in this work) are included under Selenipedium. The botanical differences between these four groups or genera are not great, indeed for all horticultural purposes they may be disregarded. There is some difference in the growth of the Tropical Asian and the Tropical American species, the former having, as a rule, shorter leaves than the latter, and while the plants from the New World have their leaves long, more or less erect, and always green, those from the Old World have in very many instances their leaves mottled with different shades of green and brown and purple. In this work all the Lady's Slipper Orchids are included under Cypripedium. It must not be forgotten that all the members of this large family are stemless, and have no pseudo-bulbs.

In every large garden where Winter-flowering plants are in request a batch of " cool " Cypripediums is as much a necessity as are Chrysanthemums, Primulas, Poinsettias, Roman Hyacinths, Euphorbias, etc., and this is so even where there is no collection of Orchids. This is sufficient to show with what ease these plants may be cultivated, and, better still, it is ample evidence of their great usefulness. *Cypripedium insigne* and its numerous varieties provide sufficient material to please most people, indeed the variations and cross-bred forms of this fine species are so abundant that their study and culture form a pleasant hobby for an amateur. *C. Leeanum* is a hybrid between *C. insigne* and *C. Spicerianum* and is a very fine plant, producing its very attractive flowers freely in the Winter. It also has numerous varieties. These two groups, *i.e. C. insigne* and *C. Leeanum* varieties, are a host in them selves, but the hybridist has been so busy during the last twelve or fifteen years that the number of Cypripediums now available for cool cultivation is very large and, naturally, the range of form and colour has been increased at the same time. *C. Boxallii, C. Charlesworthii, C. Spicerianum,* and *C. villosum* are good species to add to *C. insigne* and the hybrid *C. Leeanum,* while among the best of the cool growing hybrids the following form an excellent selection :—*C. Arthurianum, C. aureum, C. Calypso, C. Cardosoanum, C. Charlesianum, C. Colossus, C. Evelyn, C. Hera, C. Hitchinsiæ, C. Lasellei, C. Lathamianum, C. Leander, C. Menelik, C. Milo, C. Minos, C. Niobe, C. nitens, C. Norma, C. œnanthum, C. Reginæ C. Romulus, C. Savageanum, C. Schlesingerianum, C. Schrœderi, C. Simonii, C. Statterianum,* and *C. Thalia.*

The best time to pot Cypripediums is soon after they have done flowering, and it will be found that as a rule the end of February or early March will be the proper season for attending to the material wants of the cool growing section. Not all the plants will need re-potting every year, but even those that do not require this attention are improved in health and appearance if the surface of the old compost is removed carefully and new material is put in its place. Cypripedium roots are thick and fleshy ; they are also somewhat brittle. It is therefore necessary to handle the

plants carefully, and where the roots have gripped the pots the latter may have to be broken and the roots detached by means of a sharp knife. Old and large specimens, however carefully handled, are sure to lose a number of roots, especially if they are divided into several portions. In all cases where root disturbance is severe extra care in watering and shading until the plants are re-established will be amply repaid. A point worth remembering is that roots are the more easily detached from the pot if the latter is soaked in tepid water for an hour before the operation.

Use clean pots. If new pots are used they must be soaked in water for several hours previously, and then be allowed to dry. The drainage should extend to about one-third the depth of the pot. Cover this with a layer of sphagnum or peat fibre to prevent the finer portions of the potting material from working down among and blocking up the drainage. On this place a small amount of the potting compost, and then, holding the plant in the left hand, lower the roots into the pot and work the compost among and around them. Add more material and press it firmly as the work proceeds, completely covering the roots up to their attachment to the " crown " of the plant. It is neither necessary or desirable that the " crown " or " neck " of a Cypripedium should be raised above the level of the rim of the pot, nor need it be mounded up after the fashion of Odontoglossums or Cattleyas. When potting is finished the compost should be level, and half an inch or so below the rim of the pot, so as to allow an abundant supply of water to be given and ensure that it passes through the compost.

A minimum night temperature of 50 degrees, ranging to 80 degrees by day in bright warm weather, will suit the newly potted plants, and if the house and stages are frequently damped and shading is given whenever necessary, there will be little need for ventilation for a few weeks.    But as the spring advances and new roots are made and new growths appear, ventilation must be given when the temperature reaches 70 degrees, gradually increasing it as the sun heat increases.    From the middle of June to the end of August there is practically no need for artificial heat, provided the house is in an open position and has some shelter from strong prevailing winds.    When growth ceases for the year, *i.e.* when the plants cease to produce new growths and leaves, more light and air should be admitted so that the leafage may become firmer in texture and be thus able to carry the plants safely through the flowering period and the dull days of Winter.

As to the potting material.    If half a dozen experts are asked for a formula probably each will give one differing from the rest, and yet each grower may be a splendid cultivator of Cypripediums. This sort of thing puzzles a novice, but the truth of the matter is that Cypripediums are not nearly so particular over their rooting material as are many other Orchids.    The writer has received plants potted in the usual " general mixture " of peat and chopped sphagnum ; others in similar material but with fibrous loam added ; others in yellow loam only ; and others in fibrous loam, broken leaves and sand ; and in every case the plants seemed to be perfectly healthy.

Nearly all growers are agreed that Cypripediums, especially those that succeed under the cool treatment, make finer growth and flower better if placed in a more substantial compost than was formerly deemed advisable.    Moreover, out in the country, where there is purer light than in suburban districts, the heavier compost is most suitable, while a lighter compost should be used in or near towns.    A potting compost made up of two parts peat and one part each of sphagnum and fibrous loam is a good one to start with, and as the cultivator gains experience he may increase the

CYPRIPEDIUM LAIRESSEI.

amount of loam if he finds by experiment that such a procedure is desirable.  Some growers are unnecessarily "faddy" over the compost for Cypripediums, especially those who grow hardly any other kind of Orchid; but, judged by results, there is far more virtue in careful watering, and a close moist atmosphere for a few weeks after re-potting, than in a  highly specialised potting mixture.

The species and hybrids that need the heat of a stove or East Indian House thrive better in the peat, sphagnum, and loam than in a heavier material, and the writer always fancies they like a surfacing of live sphagnum, which, by the way, the cool section neither specially likes or dislikes.  Live green moss around the plants produces a tidy, healthy appearance in a house of Orchids, and most of us are willing to take some little trouble for the sake of a good appearance.  The heat loving Cypripediums need potting soon after they pass out of flower, and as they bloom at various seasons of the year there is no one special season for the work, as in the case of their cooler brethren.  Good drainage, a temperature never lower than 50 degrees, with practically no upward limit when the blinds are down and the bottom ventilators open, and abundance of moisture at the roots (except for a short time after potting) and in the atmosphere, are the chief points to bear in mind in connection with the culture of this section.  The species and hybrids referred to in the following notes and descriptions need tropical conditions unless otherwise stated.

One other little group of Cypripediums remains to be dealt with.  It consists of a few species and varieties from the Tropics of the far East, and includes *C. concolor*, *C. bellatulum*, *C. Godefroyæ*, *C. Godefroyæ leucochilum*, and *C. niveum*.  These are all dwarf growers and have rounded, fleshy flowers.  They are frequently found growing on limestone cliffs and in far more sunshine than the majority of species. Under cultivation they are not always a success, notwithstanding that many growers take any amount of pains with them.    Shallow, well-drained pots or pans suit them best, and the most approved compost consists of two parts yellow loam, and one part each of broken limestone and old oak or beach leaves, the whole pressed firmly about the roots.    The plants should be grown in the hottest part of the stove, on a shelf, or suspended near the glass, with very little shade, but with plenty of water at the roots and none given directly overhead.    There are numerous hybrids from these species and the more nearly they approach the species in growth and flower, the more nearly must the cultural conditions just indicated be followed.    But as a rule the hybrids are more easily managed than the species.

### Best Species

C. barbatum was discovered in 1840 in the Malay Peninsula, near Malacca.    In the following year it flowered for the first time under cultivation with the Messrs Loddiges, of Hackney.    The species is found in most collections, but as a rule it is not seen in such good condition now as it was twenty years ago ; this is probably due to the introduction of so many hybrids and the general inclination to cultivate these to the exclusion of species.    A year or two ago, when visiting the mining villages of Prudhoe and West Wylam, near Newcastle, the writer saw some excellent specimens of this old Orchid in the glass houses of the enthusiastic miners who make a hobby of gardening, and ride their hobby hard and well.    The flowers are of medium size and the rounded dorsal sepal is white, with a green base, and veinings of deep purple.    The petals are green, shading to purple at the apex, hairy along the margin, and with several small, blackish warts along the upper edge.    The lip is dull purple.    The variety C. B. Crossii

VARIETIES OF CYPRIPEDIUM INSIGNE.

SENI HAREFIELD HALL.    C. INSIGNE SANDERÆ.    INSIGNE (TYPI).

is of dwarfer habit and has brighter flowers than the type; other good varieties are C. B. NIGRUM and C. B. SUPERBUM.

C. BELLATULUM is found in Siam, but, for a long time after its introduction in 1888 by Messrs H. Low & Co., its habitat was unknown. Of dwarf growth, with thick leaves that are curiously bilobed at the apex, purple beneath, and mottled with light, greyish green on deep green above, this is one of the most interesting species. The rounded flowers are about three inches across, rounded, fleshy, and borne on a very short stem. The ground colour is white or pale yellow, but this is freely spotted with dark maroon-purple, the markings being very heavy in some flowers and much smaller in others. The lip is comparatively small, and is much less marked than the petals. The rare and beautiful C. BELLATULUM ALBUM is pure white and unspotted. Both the type and the variety are summer flowering.

C. BOXALLII comes from Burmah, where it was discovered about 1877 by Mr Boxall, when collecting for Messrs H. Low & Co. In growth and shape of flower it closely resembles *C. villosum*, and for a long time it was regarded as a variety of the latter species. The chief point of difference between C. BOXALLII and *C. villosum* is that the former has a pure white apex to the dorsal sepal, and from the centre to the base of that sepal there are numerous and often confluent spots of dark blackish purple. C. BOXALLII shows a good deal of variation, however, and in some forms it closely approaches *C. villosum* in colour. It is a species easily managed in a cool house. A very striking and distinct variety is C. B. ATRATUM; in this the dorsal sepal is almost black and the rest of the flower is of deeper colour than usual, and richly burnished.

C. CALLOSUM is a handsome plant even when not in flower, as its leaves, about nine inches long, are prettily mottled and tesselated with light green on a deep green ground. The large blooms appear in Spring or early Summer, and are each carried at the end of a stout stem, fifteen or eighteen inches high. On the broad white dorsal sepal there are deep wine-purple veins, curving a little from base to apex, and short veins alternate with long ones; at the base of the sepal there is some green shading. This Siamese species is essentially one for the warm house and it is altogether a desirable plant. The albino variety, C. c. SANDERÆ, has the white parts very pure and all the parts that are coloured in the type are light apple green in the variety.

C. CAUDATUM invariably attracts attention when in bloom because of the great length of its petals, and the most interesting point about these is that when a flower opens the petals are three inches long, but during the following week they elongate at the rate of two inches or more each day. Eighteen or twenty inches is a common length for the petals to reach, and a total length of thirty inches is on record. As the spikes carry two or three flowers, occasionally four, a large specimen with several spikes of expanded flowers presents a wonderful sight. C. CAUDATUM hails from Peru and is not difficult to cultivate in a warm, moist house. It has robust green leaves that often reach a length of fifteen inches. The flowers are large and the lower sepal is larger than the dorsal one; they are both creamy white, with regular, bright yellow-green veins. The elongated, pendulous petals are brownish-crimson, shading to yellow-green at the base; they are also narrow and ribbon-like. The bronze-green lip is shell-shaped, veined with darker green, and the infolded side lobes are whitish, lightly spotted with purple. There are several varieties of C. CAUDATUM, the most important ones being *C. C. Lindenii*, in which the lip has become petaloid, and elongated; C. c. LUXEM-BOURG, with bright yellow sepals and purplish petals; C. c.

CYPRIPEDIUM FAIRRIEANUM.

WALLISII, smaller and paler than the type; and C. c. WARSCIWICZII, with shorter, darker foliage, and rosy-flushed flowers.

C. CHARLESWORTHII, a dwarf Burmese species, will thrive under the conditions that prove suitable for *C. insigne* and its varieties.    Few Orchids have created so great a sensation as C. CHARLESWORTHII; in 1903 it first flowered in this country, and when exhibited by Messrs Charlesworth, Shuttleworth & Co., of Heaton, Bradford, its large, flat, deep rose-coloured dorsal sepal at once attracted attention and suggested great possibilities to the hybridists.    For a little while it was a rare plant, but other importations were received, notably by Messrs Hugh Low & Co., and plants were sold at public auction during the following year, so that within twelve months of the time the species first came before the public it was to be found in nearly all the leading Orchid collections in the land.    The discoverer was Mr R. Moore, who found it in the Shan States, twenty-five miles south-west of Lake Inle, at an elevation of 5000 feet above sea level, and on limestone hills.    It was subsequently found at places scores of miles from the spot where Mr Moore discovered it.    The petals and lip of C. CHARLESWORTHII are yellow-green, heavily shaded with brown, and the broad dorsal sepal shows considerable variation.    This may be deep rose or it may be pure white, though the latter is rare.    Sometimes the sepal appears to be white, suffused and veined with rose.    It is a charming little Orchid, rarely more than nine inches high.    Grown under the very coolest conditions that will suffice for *C. insigne* it grows slowly, but if given the temperature of a warm greenhouse, *i.e.* a minimum of 50 degrees, it grows better and flowers freely.

C. CURTISII was discovered by the writer's relative and name-sake, in Sumatra, when collecting for Messrs Jas. Veitch & Sons, Chelsea, in 1882.    The large bold flowers are produced in late Spring and Summer, and are generally to be seen in considerable numbers at the great annual Temple Show in London. A con spicuous feature of the flower is the large, full, helmet-shaped lip, of a dull purple-brown colour. The green dorsal sepal has a white margin, and is regularly and heavily veined with dark green that shades to purple towards the apex. The petals are whitish, or pale purple, veined with green, and have raised black spots along the margin. They are curiously deflexed and reach to about the end of the lip. C. CURTISII has handsome leaves in which two shades of green are prettily intermixed. The species should be grown in a stove temperature, and it is then easily managed. Some of the Prudhoe miners grow it very well.

C. FAIRRIEANUM is a lowly species, rarely exceeding eight inches high even when in bloom. The flowers are small, about three inches across from the tip of the dorsal sepal to the end of the lip, but the beautiful rose-purple veinings on the white ground of the upper sepal make it very attractive, and the petals, deflexed and then upturned at the tip, moustache fashion, give the flower an interesting appearance. These are pale green with purple veins and have black hairs along the margin. The lip is brownish green with purple veins. For many years C. FAIRRIEANUM became rarer and rarer in cultivation and its rarity, the absence of importations or knowledge of its habitat, together with the fact that the hybrids derived from it were of great value, all lent a wonderful interest to the species. At last, just when hybridists seemed to have given up all hope of ever receiving imported plants, and when the few living cultivated plants were beyond price, the species was rediscovered, importations followed each other, and now C. FAIRRIEANUM is found in almost every collection and in some quantity. In 1857 flowers of C. FAIRRIEANUM were sent to Kew from a garden in Somersetshire, and also from Mr Parker's

Nursery at Upper Holloway, and in October of the same year a flowering plant was exhibited before the Royal Horticultural Society by Mr Fairrie, of Aigburth, Liverpool.   Dr Lindley described the species and named it after Mr Fairrie.   It was supposed that all the plants thus represented had been imported from Assam and offered with other Orchids at one of the sales at Stevens' Rooms.   It is also stated that M. Van Houtte received some plants from Bhotan.   In 1880 the Messrs Veitch exhibited a plant before the Royal Horticultural Society and gained a First Class Certificate for it.   From that time onwards practically nothing was heard of C. FAIRRIEANUM until almost half a century had elapsed since its introduction, and then, in 1905, some plants were sent to the Calcutta Botanic Gardens, and others eventually reached Kew.   Many were the rumours concerning a re-discovery of C. FAIRRIEANUM, and the Orchid world was in a state of excitement.   Later in the year Messrs Sander and Sons, St Albans, sold plants privately, and over a hundred were sold in the auction rooms in Cheapside.   The Kew plants flowered, and in the Autumn flowering plants were exhibited in London and all doubt as to the identity of the plant was at rest.   The long lost Orchid was re-discovered by Mr G. S. Searight, who found it high up in the valley of the Torsa River, in the Chumbi district of Western Bhotan.   Wherever C. *insigne* is well grown there should be no difficulty in managing C. FAIRRIEANUM under similar treatment. *C. vexillarium, C. Juno, C. Arthurianum, C. Reginæ, C. Schrœderi, C. Niobe,* and *C. Edwardii* are a few of the pretty hybrids descended from C. FAIRRIEANUM, while there are numerous secondary hybrids of considerable garden value.

C. GODEFROYÆ is a beautiful, low-growing Orchid intermediate between *C. niveum* and *C. concolor,* and probably all three are but geographical forms of one species.   Mr C. Curtis, when at Pinang, repeatedly collected these Cypripediums as well as *C. bellatulum* when on botanising excursions, and never found any two of them growing together. *C. niveum* is found in the Langkawi group of islands; from the island about Tongkah or from the neighbouring mainland of the Malay Peninsula, and even from the Siamese side comes C. GODEFROYÆ and its variety C. G. LEUCOCHILUM; while from the Moulmein district and Lower Burmah *C. concolor* is found. *C. bellatulum* hails from what may be called the Mandalay region. *C. niveum* also occurs in the Tambilan Islands that lie to the west of Sarawak, and it was here it was discovered soon after its first discovery (presumably) in the Langkawi Islands. But this is somewhat of a digression. C. GODEFROYÆ was introduced by M. Godefroy, of Argenteuil, but it was discovered about 1876 by an old Kewite named Murton, though the plants he collected never reached Europe, as Murton died before they could be despatched, and Mr Alabaster, in whose care they were placed, was taken ill, and so the plants were lost. But Alabaster found other plants and sent them to M. Godefroy. The flowers are white, sometimes yellowish; the upper sepal and the deflexed petals are freely spotted with purple, and the lip is sprinkled with tiny purple dots. The form of the flower is better than that of the pale yellow, purple dotted *C. concolor*, but scarcely so good as that of *C. niveum*, while in substance, size and heavy markings C. GODEFROYÆ falls short of *C. bellatulum*, though it is far more elegant than the latter. C. GODEFROYÆ should be grown in the same way as *C. bellatulum* and *C. niveum*. C. GODEFROYÆ LEUCOCHILUM differs from the type in having a pure white lip, and it is a very desirable plant.

C. INSIGNE, probably the most popular and widely grown Orchid, was discovered by Dr Wallich in North-East India and sent to England about 1819-1820. At a later date it was found

CYPRIPEDIUM ŒNANTHUM SUPERBUM.

in quantity on the Khasia Hills, and in more modern times it has been found to have a still wider range. It is a very variable species, but usually it has a broadly oval dorsal sepal which is green along the centre and base, and white at the upper part; the green area is more or less freely spotted with purple or purple-brown, and if the spots extend into the white area they are then bright purple. The stiff, spreading petals are light green with brown or dull purple veins, and the lip is light green, often quite yellow-green, shaded with brown. The flower is bold, and is finely posed on a stout stem, from eight to twelve inches high, and it shines as though beautifully polished or varnished. Few flowers last so long in a cut state as those of C. INSIGNE. In some Orchid collections C. INSIGNE and its varieties are made a fine feature. Mr G. F. Moore, of Chardwar, Bourton-on-the-Water, has a particularly fine collection of varieties, the great majority bearing distinctive names. The late Mr Drewett O. Drewett, of Riding-mill-on-Tyne, also brought together a very interesting set of C. INSIGNE varieties, and for many years he worked for the improvement of the species by crossing and re-crossing the best forms, and selecting the finest resulting seedlings. He was particularly successful, and some of his best results are C. I. EMPEROR, and C. I. GEORGE RENWICK. The largest of the C. INSIGNE varieties are C. I. HAREFIELD HALL and C. I. FRANCIS WELLESLEY. Other notable varieties are C. I. MAULEI, C. I. PUNCTATUM-VIOLACEUM or CHANTINII. But there are crowds of named varieties, though comparatively few of them are in general cultivation. Besides those mentioned, and others with bright colouring and distinct spotting, there is a group of varieties in which the absence of colour and spotting is the mark of perfection; these are albinos, or nearly so. The finest of this group is C. I. SANDERÆ, which has primrose-yellow flowers with a white apex to the upper sepal.

Among other charming varieties composing this section, but scarcely so beautiful as C. I. SANDERÆ, are C. I. COBBIANUM, C. I. ERNESTII, C. I. LAURA KIMBALL, C. I. LINDENII, C. MAC-FARLANEI, and C. I. SANDERIANUM. C. INSIGNE (or its varieties) has been one parent of about sixty hybrids, including C. FOWLERÆ, C. HITCHINSÆ, C. ÆSON, C. ARTHURIANUM, C. ŒNANTHUM, C. GEM, C. VENUS, C. MILO, C. MAGNIFICUM, C. THALIA, C. NITENS, etc.

C. LAWRENCEANUM is a very fine Lady's Slipper Orchid and one that needs and thoroughly merits stove treatment. It was discovered in North Borneo by the late Mr F. W. Burbidge, in 1878, and named after Sir Trevor Lawrence, Bt., the President of the Royal Horticultural Society. The flowers are often five inches across and are carried on stems about eighteen inches high. The broad dorsal sepal is white with deep, rich purple veins, half of which are shorter than the rest and alternate with them. The out-spread petals are green, tipped with purple, and have marginal hairs and blackish warts. A few varietal forms have occurred, some remarkable for the richness of their colouring, but the one that shows the greatest divergence from the type is the albino, C. LAWRENCEANUM HYEANUM. In this all the purple colouring has disappeared, and except for the white ground of the dorsal sepal the flower is light apple-green. C. LAWRENCEANUM has been freely used as a parent, and, in combination with other species, it has yielded *C. Lawrebel, C. Maudiæ* (*C. L. Hyeanum* was the parent in this case), *C. concolawre, C. Gowerianum, C. gigas, C. Aphrodite, C. Euryale,* etc.

C. NIVEUM, the dainty little species from the tropics of the far East, is one of the gems of the family. Its rounded white flowers always attract attention, and the tiny dots of purple that group themselves towards the base of the sepal and petals add to its

CYPRIPEDIUM THALIA.

beauty. It was introduced by Messrs J. Veitch & Sons, in 1868, but its habitat was not known until Forsterman collected it in the Langkawi Islands for Messrs Sander & Sons, many years later. Other references to C. NIVEUM will be found under the notes on *C. bellatulum* and *C. Godefroyæ*.

C. PURPURATUM is a beautiful, but unfortunately a very rare species. It is a native of Hong Kong and the adjacent Chinese mainland, and was introduced by Mr Knight, of Chelsea, as long ago as 1836. It is a dwarf plant with short, thick, tesselated leaves, and carries its flowers about six inches high. As a rule the flowers are about three inches across, the dorsal sepal being white with a green base, and very regularly marked with purple-brown stripes. The petals are purple, sometimes shaded with crimson and veined with green; the lip is purplish, with darker veins C. PURPURATUM is a very pretty plant, but it does not seem to take kindly to cultivation. An intermediate temperature suits it best.

C. ROTHSCHILDEANUM ranks among the noblest of Cypridediums as it is a strong grower and bears large flowers on tall spikes. The broad, glossy green leaves are often two feet long, while the reddish purple spike is sometimes a yard high, and may carry as many as six blooms. To Messrs Sander & Sons is given the credit of introducing this species from New Guinea in 1887. The upper and lower sepals are nearly equal in size and colouring; the ground colour is greenish yellow, and on this are longitudinal stripes of blackish purple. The long petals stand out horizontally and taper gradually to a point; they are yellowish, striped with dark purple and spotted with the same colour, the spots being most numerous towards the base. The lip large and curiously elongated; dull brownish yellow with brown-purple veins. There is very little variation in C. ROTHSCHILDEANUM except that some plants seem to be naturally more free flowering than others. The

Northaw House variety is a fine example of this freedom; this belongs to J. B. Joel, Esq., Northaw House, Childwickbury, St Albans, and when exhibited in May 1910, it carried six spikes, with a total of thirty-two flowers and buds.  A stove temperature is necessary for this splendid Orchid.

C. SPICERIANUM is a species which the hybridist has taken full advantage of, and crossed with *C. insigne* it has given us the beautiful and extremely useful *C. Leeanum*, while *C. Minos*, *C. Calypso*, *C. Moensiæ*, *C. Niobe*, *C. aureum*, *C. Statterianum*, and *C. Lathamianum* are also among its important children.  It was in the autumn of 1878 that Mr H. Spicer, of Godalming, sent a flower of this species to Messrs J. Veitch & Sons, but he could not tell the origin of the plant.  The Chelsea firm subsequently secured the whole stock, and the species was named after Mr Spicer. For a little while C. SPICERIANUM was rare and expensive, but before long it was discovered in Assam by collectors sent out by the Messrs Low and Messrs Sander, and so it became a popular and widely grown Orchid.  C. SPICERIANUM is a plant of neat habit, and carries its flowers on stems about nine inches high. Each flower is rather more than three inches across, and has a bold, white dorsal sepal, with its lower margins reflexed.  This segment is green at the base, and down the keeled centre is a deep crimson-purple band.  The deflexed petals point forward a little, have strongly undulate margins and are light green, speckled with purple, and have a central reddish line.  The lip is very shapely, brown, shaded with red.  C. SPICERIANUM is a capital plant for inclusion in a collection of cool Orchids.

C. STONEI, a strong-growing stove species, was discovered about 1860 by Sir Hugh Low, and it was introduced to cultivation by Messrs H. Low & Co., of Clapton.  It first flowered with Mr J. Day, who had a fine collection of Orchids at Tottenham, and

CYPRIPEDIUM MAUDIÆ.

was named after his gardener. It is a native of Sarawak, Borneo. From an importation secured by the Messrs Low in 1863, Mr Day purchased a number of plants, and one of these flowered in 1867 and proved to be a far finer thing than the type, and so far as is known no other plant of this novelty—C. STONEI PLATYTÆNIUM —has since been imported. From it a few small plants were propagated, but it was not until the disposal of Mr Day's collection by auction in 1889 that this wonderful Orchid really came into the market. The strongest plants were purchased by Sir Trevor Lawrence, Bt., and the late Baron Sir Henry Schroder, and at the time of writing there are few examples of it outside the Dell and Burford Lodge collections. It is generally understood that no less than £1000 was paid for the finest specimen at the sale referred to. C. STONEI has a white, crimson-striped dorsal sepal, and a lower sepal of almost equal size and colour; the petals are quite narrow and about six inches long, pale yellow at the base, gradually shading to dull crimson at the apex, and spotted with brownish crimson. The lip projects as in *C. Rothschildeanum*, and is very attractive, the colour being rose, with reticulating veins of crimson. In the variety PLATYTÆNIUM the flowers are in every way glorified; they are larger, and the petals are much broader, while the colouring is more brilliant, the petals being heavily spotted with deep crimson almost to the base. *C. Morganiæ* is one of the best of the hybrids derived from *C. Stonei*. There are a few hybrids from *C. Stonei platytænium, i.e. C. platycolor, C. concolor* being the other parent; *C. Morganiæ langleyense*, and *C. James H. Veitch*, the latter having *C. Curtisii* as its seed parent, and therefore really a varietal form of *C. Constance (C. Curtisii x C. Stonei)*.

C. SUPERBIENS has had many names, and as it has been described as *C. barbatum Veitchii* and *C. barbatum supurbum*, some indication of its general appearance will be gained from these titles.

The white dorsal sepal is lightly veined with green, and the deflexed petals are of similar colouring but have a large number of black warts on them, these being smallest and most numerous towards the base. The helmet-shaped lip is dull purple with crimson markings. C. SUPERBIENS is a summer flowering stove species, and even when not in flower it is a handsome plant because of the variegation of its leafage. The species was found at the southern end of the Malay Peninsula.

C. VILLOSUM concludes a selection of eighteen species, all of which are well worthy of cultivation. It is a fine Orchid, but now there is a craze for Cypripediums that have a flattened dorsal sepal, of rounded outline, it is less popular than formerly. C. VILLOSUM was discovered by Thomas Lobb in Moulmein, and introduced to cultivation in 1853. It comes from a considerable elevation, and it will thrive under the same conditions as *C. insigne* where this is grown to perfection and not subjected to the very cool treatment it sometimes receives. The species grows vigorously and has leaves from twelve to eighteen inches long. The bold flowers are five or six inches across, and therefore among the largest found in the genus. The flower stems do not grow so stiffly erect as in the case of *C. insigne* and some other species, but are bent over a little by the weight of the flower. The dorsal sepal does not conform to the canons of floriculture that find favour with so many growers; it hoods over somewhat, and the lateral margins are considerably reflexed from centre to base; the apex is white, and below this is a green area, but the larger part of this segment is rich purple-brown, the colour deepening towards the base. The petals are quite narrow at the base but quickly broaden out and are very prominent and attractive, brownish yellow with purple veins. The lip is also brownish yellow with a brighter yellow margin to the mouth. C. VILLOSUM varies

CATTLEYA HARDYANA.

considerably, and one of the finest forms is named C. v. AUREUM. This has flowers in which the purple colouring has been almost obliterated, and the yellow shade highly developed and toned with pale brown.

## BEST HYBRIDS

If the reader will remember that there are about eight hundred hybrid Cypripediums, then some idea of the difficulty encountered in making a small selection will be appreciated. Further, tastes differ so much that it is hardly possible the selection will find general favour. The first selection made consisted of no fewer than eighty hybrids, or about ten per cent. of the whole. A further reduction brought the number down to five and twenty, and though all of these are not what a modern raiser and Cypripedium specialist would consider first class, they are all good growers and flower well under fair treatment; in other words, they are good garden plants. In dealing with these hybrids some consideration must be given to the needs of the dominant parent; thus if *C. bellatulum* is one parent then a modification of the treatment accorded that species must be afforded. In every case the hybrids in the following selection have been raised a number of times, and in different establishments, and therefore in some instances particularly fine varieties of the parent species have been used for breeding purposes. This at once suggests the possibility of a wide difference in the progeny, and so it comes about that while an ordinarily good form of a hybrid may be purchased for a few shillings, an abnormally fine one may cost as many pounds sterling.

Twenty-five of the finest Cypripedium hybrids selected for their beauty of form and colour, according to the latest decree of Orchid fashion and with some regard for their rarity, could only be obtained by the expenditure of a small fortune. The catalogue

of a well-known firm is at hand, and a glance over its pages reveals
the fact that fifteen of the finest and rarest Cypripedium hybrids
are only to be obtained by an expenditure of a trifle less than
£500, and the plants would be small ones at the price.    Many
of the rarest hybrids, or fine varietal forms of them, are not
catalogued at all, simply because only one plant is known, and it
is either kept for stock purposes or has passed into the possession
of some wealthy amateur at a price that makes one's mouth water.
On the score of expense, however, the selection here given affords
little ground for complaint, as may be gathered from the fact that
the writer has examples of nearly all of them in his own modest
collection.    Descriptions are not given, because as a general rule
the hybrids show the chief characteristics of their parents, and, as
indicated above, there is a good deal of variation between certain
limits, due to the variation in the species concerned.

C. ARTHURIANUM is one of the earlier hybrids, derived from
*C. Fairrieanum* and *C. insigne*.    C. AUREUM (*C. nitens* ×
*C. Spicerianum*), is a bold and beautiful hybrid, and some of its
finer varietal forms are C. A. CYRUS, C. A. HEBE, C. A. MARIE
CLOSON, C. A. ŒDIPPE, and C. A. VIRGINALE.    C. CALYPSO
(*C. Boxallii* × *C. Spicerianum*), is another pretty and useful Winter
flowering hybrid, and a splendid grower; C. C. OAKWOOD VAR. and
C. C. FLAMINGO are two of the best forms, but the type is good
enough for anyone.    C. CHARLESIANUM (*C. Leeanum* × *C. nitens*),
was first raised in 1894, and may be regarded as a glorified form
of *C. Leeanum*, indeed it was once named *C. Leeanum superbum*.
C. COLOSSUS (*C. nitens* × *C. villosum*), is a bold, handsome Winter
flowerer, that is perhaps better known under its later but not
correct title of *Cypripedium J. Howes*; it combines a good deal
of the size and polish of *C. Boxallii*, with the colouring of *C.
insigne*.    C. EVELYN (*C. Calypso* × *C. Leeanum*), appears to have

CYPRIPEDIUM INSIGNE SANDERÆ.

been raised in America about 1900; it is a very fine Winter
flowering Orchid, and, through *C. Calypso*, it has a good deal of
the form of *C. Boxallii*.   C. MRS W. MOSTYN is from the same
parentage, but C. EVELYN is the prior name.   C. GIGAS (*C.
Harrisianum* x *C. Lawrenceanum*), needs moderately warm treatment, and has a bright bold flower; C. G. CORNDEANI and C. G.
EMPEROR OF INDIA are especially fine forms.   C. GERMINYANUM
(*C. hirsutissimum* x *C. villosum*), has the form of the latter and
a good deal of the brightness of the former parent.   C.
GOWERIANUM (*C. Curtisii* x *C. Lawrenceanum*), is a bold and
effective hybrid from two large flowering species; it needs a warm
house.   C. GRANDE (*C. caudatum* x *C. longifolium*), is a very
strong-growing hybrid belonging to the Phragmopedilum section
of the genus, and one that must be grown in a warm house; it
has long tail-like petals and shows the influence of *C. caudatum* in
a marked degree; in the variety, C. G. ATRATUM, the colouring is
deeper than in the type, while in the variety, C. G. MACROCHILUM,
the lip is unusually well developed.

C. HARRISIANUM (*C. barbatum* x *C. villosum*), the first hybrid
in the genus, is still thoroughly worthy of inclusion in any collection.   C. HERA is one of the very best of the cool section, and its
parentage (*C. Boxallii* x *C. Leeanum*) will at once suggest its worth
and appearance; it is extremely variable, and is well represented in
most collections under the varietal names of C. ADRASTUS and
C. EURYADES.   C. HITCHINSIÆ (*C. Charlesworthii* x *C. insigne*), is
another useful, attractive, and easily-grown hybrid, occasionally seen
labelled *C. bingleyense*.   C. LATHAMIANUM, one of the earlier
hybrids, is from a good stock (*C. Spicerianum* x *C. villosum*), and
it has been raised repeatedly at home and abroad since Mr Latham
raised it at Birmingham.   C. LEANDER (*C. Leeanum* x *C. villosum*),
has also been raised frequently at home, on the Continent, and in

America, and has received a number of names; the CAMBRIDGE
LODGE variety and C. L. THOMPSONI are both good.   C. LEEANUM
(*C. insigne* x *C. Spicerianum*), is one of the most popular cool
Orchids, and one of the best for a small collection ; owing to the
wide variation of *C. insigne* it has been possible to obtain considerable variety in this hybrid, but all are good, free flowering, and
bloom during the Winter, when the large white area of the dorsal
sepal is very attractive in conjunction with the green and brown of
the rest of the flower; distinct varieties are: C. L. ALBERTIANUM,
C. L. CLINKABERRYANUM, C. L. GIGANTEUM, and C. L. SUPERBUM.
C. MAUDIÆ (*C. Lawrenceanum Hyeanum* x *C. callosum Sanderæ*),
is rather expensive as compared with others in this selection, but it
is too good to be omitted, especially as in a warm house it grows
so freely and blooms regularly, giving large flowers that are white
and pale apple-green; the coloured form of this hybrid, derived
from the species instead of from the albino varieties, did not appear
until several years after the original C. MAUDIÆ.    C. MILO,
(*C. insigne* x *C. œnanthum*), was raised in 1894, and is a dwarf
grower ; the HEATON variety and the WESTONBIRT variety of C.
MILO are both of fine form and colour.    C. MORGANIÆ (*C. Stonei*
x *C. superbiens*), is a splendid free-growing and free-flowering
hybrid that carries several large flowers on each spike ; many years
ago it used to be grown particularly well in the Paradise Nurseries
at Holloway, and at almost every season of the year plants could be
found in bloom at that establishment.   C. NIOBE (*C. Fairrieanum*
x *C. Spicerianum*), is a delighful little hybrid with a good deal of
purple colouring, and it is one of the best of the *C. Fairrieanum*
crosses.    C. NITENS (*C. insigne* x *C. villosum*), is an effective
combination of two fine old species ; it grows well, and flowers
freely in the winter, and its finer varieties are C. N. MAGNIFICUM,
C. N. SALLIERI, and C. N. SUPERBUM.    C. ŒNANTHUM (*C.*

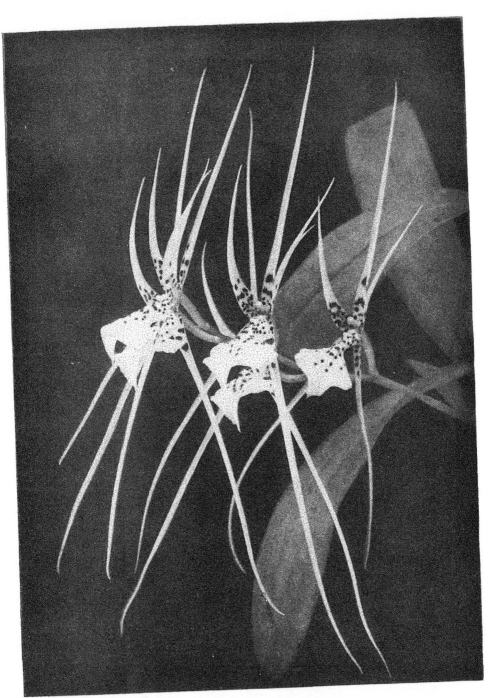

BRASSIA VERRUCOSA.

*Harrisianum* x *C. insigne*), is another of the older hybrids, but one that is not to be despised for that reason ; this cross has probably been raised more times than any other, and the names given to the progeny of the species indicated is startling; C. Œ. SUPERBUM, C. Œ. GALATEA and C. Œ. MDME. COFFINET are good varieties. C. SIMONII (*C. insigne* x *C. Leeanum*), is perhaps better known as C. ACTEUS, a name that represents a very fine form of this variable hybrid. C. THALIA (*C. insigne* x *Schrœderi*), is very fine and a much better grower than the handsome, brightly-coloured *C. Schrœderi* ; four species are concerned in its production, *i.e.* *C. insigne*, *C. barbatum*, *C. Fairrieanum*, and *C. villosum*. C. THALIA variety MRS FRANCIS WELLESLEY, is one of the most handsome of all Cypripediums, no matter what their class. C. TRIUMPHANS (*C. nitens* x *C. œnanthum*), adds one more to the twenty-five selected hybrids; it is of very mixed parentage, but gives a bold, bright flower.

### OTHER SPECIES

Among the Cypripedium species not hitherto described there are several of sufficient merit to justify their inclusion in a collection where there is ample room, and where the species and hybrids already selected are well represented. C. ARGUS, from the Philippine Islands, is remarkable for its handsome foliage and the bold, blackish warts on its petals. C. CHAMBERLAINIANUM comes from Sumatra, and bears its flowers in succession on a gradually elongating spike; it is a very distinct species, and has its petals curiously curled or twisted, one in the opposite direction to the other. C. CILIOLARE bears a considerable resemblance to *C. super-biens* ; it comes from the Philippine Islands and flowers in the Spring. C. CONCOLOR belongs to the *C. bellatulum* group, and is referred to under *C. Godefroyæ*. C. DAYANUM is a good and rather variable species, first found on Mt. Kina Balu, in Borneo. C. DRURYI is from Southern India and is notable for the broad median band of blackish purple down each petal and the dorsal sepal. C. HAYNAL-DIANUM is another species from the Philippine Islands, and like those that hail from thence needs a warm house; the purple shading on its flowers gives it a distinction and it almost always bears several flowers on a spike. C. HIRSUTISSIMUM was found in the Khasia Hills; all its segments are margined with hairs, the petals are much undulated and the dorsal sepal is densely dotted with purple. C. HOOKERÆ has a good deal of yellow-green colouring, but its flowers are comparatively small. C. LOWII, from Borneo, bears several of its yellow-green, purple-stained flowers on a spike, in the Spring months. C. MASTERSIANUM is a Javanese species that was little known until its re-importation a few years ago by Messrs Sander and Sons; it has a bright green dorsal sepal, with yellowish white margin to the dorsal sepal, the latter being very large in proportion to the size of the flower. C. PARISHII is a distinct species with long, twisted, green ribbon-like petals, and a prominent lip. C. SANDERIANUM is a Bornean species that has long, narrow, pendulous petals, but otherwise it suggests a miniature C. *Rothschildeanum*. C. TONSUM has polished flowers in which white, green, and purple, are the principal colours. C. VENUSTUM, from North-west India, used to be largely grown, and it is still worth cultivation because of its freedom of flowering, its green, warted flowers and its handsomely variegated foliage.

From the Phragmopedilum section three species may be selected as worthy of cultivation if space permits. These are C. LINDLEYANUM, C. LONGIFOLIUM, and C. SCHLIMII. C. LONGIFOLIUM is a very strong grower and needs a stove temperature; its flowers are borne on a tall spike and follow each other in steady succession

CYPRIPEDIUM LEANDER THOMPSONI.

over a long period. C. SCHLIMII succeeds in the cool house and
has neat, pretty flowers that are white, shaded with pink or pale
purple. This species is remarkable because it is self-fertilising, and
is one parent of a series of hybrids that were formerly in high
favour, but, as a consequence of their large growth and the fact
that the flowers do not last long when cut, and are so liable to
damage if bruised, they have fallen from favour.

## OTHER HYBRIDS

In any prominent race, horse or foot, there are invariably
a number of entrants of whom it is reported they "also ran."
But not seldom some of these are in many ways as good as the
winners and often indeed prove the better over a period of years.
So it is with many of the hybrid Cypripediums. A hybrid may
not be regarded as tip-top, but there comes a time when the
opportunity for crossing splendid varieties of the parent species
occurs and is taken advantage of, with the result that the progeny
is first class and is received with acclamation. On such occasion,
however, the new comer is generally given a name altogether
different to that of the original hybrid, instead of a varietal one.
In the following list some of the very finest Cypripediums are included, but it would have been useless to place them in the former
selection because they are not obtainable in the ordinary course of
business, or only at high prices.

C. ÆSON (*C. insigne* x *C. Druryi*); C. ALLANIANUM (*C.
Curtisii* x *C. Spicerianum*); C. AYLINGII (*C. ciliolare* x *C. niveum*),
C. WINIFRED HOLLINGTON is a fine form; C. BALLANTINEI (*C.
Fairrieanum* x *C. purpuratum*), C. B. WESTFIELD *var.* is a brilliantly
coloured form; C. BERKELEYANUM (*C. bellatulum* x *C. Boxallii*),
C. BEEKMANI is a large variety raised on the Continent; C.
BUCHANIANUM (*C. Druryi* x *C. Spicerianum*); C. CARDOSOANUM (*C.

*barbatum* × *C. Leeanum*); C. CASTLEANUM (*C. hirsutissimum* × *C. superbiens*); C. CHAPMANII (*C. bellatulum* × *C. Curtisii*), the varieties C. C. MAGNIFICUM and C. C. SUPERBUM are in advance of the type; C. CHLORONEURUM (*C. Harrisianum* × *C. venustum*); C. CONCO-LAWRE (*C. concolor* × *C. Lawrenceanum*); C. Constance (*C. Curtisii* × *C. Stonei*), in the variety named C. JAMES H. VEITCH, *C. Stonei platytænium* was the pollen parent; C. CYCNIDES (*C. bellatulum* × *C. Swanianum*), the variety C. WILLIAM LLOYD is very deeply coloured, and shapely; C. CYMATODES (*C. Curtisii* × *C. superbiens*), C. BEECHENSE is a fine form; C. DOM CARLOS (*C. Godefroyæ* × *C. Lawrenceanum*), the variety REX is an especially good one; C. DICKSONIANUM (*C. Hera* × *C. villosum*); C. EDWARDII (*C. Fairrieanum* × *C. superbiens*); C. EDWARDIANUM (*C. nitens* × *C. Rothschildeanum*), is a fine hybrid that was shown as *C. King Edward VII.*; C. ETTYI (*C. Godefroyæ* × *C. insigne*), is a rare and beautiful hybrid, best known by its varietal form named C. QUEEN OF ITALY; C. EUCHARIS (*C. insigne* × *C. Lawrenceanum*); C. FIGARO (*C. ænanthum* × *C. Spicerianum*), is a bold flower very frequently exhibited as C. TITYUS; C. FOWLERÆ (*C. Chamberlainianum* × *C. insigne*), originally exhibited as *C. Miss Louise Fowler*; C. GIGANTEUM (*C. Harrisianum* × *C. nitens*); C. GODSEFFIANUM (*C. Boxallii* × *C. hirsutissimum*), originally raised by Mr Cookson, and well represented by its varietal forms C. JUPITER and C. OTHELLO; C. GRAVESÆ (*C. Argus* × *C. niveum*), the inverse cross is commonly known as C. RUTH AYLING.

C. HELENA (*C. bellatulum* × *C. insigne*), a charming hybrid of which C. HELEN II. is a fine form; C. IO *C. Argus* × *C. Lawrenceanum*), a striking hybrid with petals that are very heavily warted in the variety GRANDE; C. JERNINGHAMIÆ (*C. Spicerianum* × *C. Winnianum*), a very fine hybrid whose parentage

is only surmised so far; C. Juno (*C. callosum* x *C. Fairrieanum*);
C. Lasellei (*C. Leeanum* x *C. Schlesingerianum*), a fine Orchid,
especially as represented by Lt.-Col. Sir G. Holford's magnificent
variety, exhibited as C. Alcibiades magnificum; C. Lairessei
(*C. Curtisii* x *C. Rothschildeanum*), an especially free flowering
hybrid, bearing several flowers on a spike, and generally cultivated
under the title of *Cypripedium A. de Lairesse*; C. Lawrebel
(*C. bellatulum* x *C. Lawrenceanum*), one of the best of the *bellatulum*
hybrids; C. Leonæ (*C. callosum* x *C. insigne*); C. Little Gem
(*C. Harrisianum* x *C. Schrœderi*), a very showy little hybrid, the
Westfield variety being particularly rich in colour; C. Mabeliæ
(*C. Rothschildeanum* x *C. superbiens*), a handsome hybrid, best
known under its varietal forms named C. Lord Derby and C. W.
R. Lee, Sander's var.; C. Measuresianum (*C. venustum* x *C.
villosum*); C. Menelik (*C. Boxallii* x *C. Calypso*); C. Minnie
(*C. concolor* x *C. Curtisii*), known also as *C. Minnie Ames*, and
*C. Annie Ayling*; C. Minos (*C. Arthurianum* x *C. Spicerianum*),
the varieties C. M. Youngii and C. M. Westfield var. are both
good; C. Olenus (*C. bellatulum* x *C. ciliolare*), a fine hybrid, also
well known as *C. Gertrude Hollington*; C. Opoixiæ (*C. niveum*
x *C. ciliolare*), formely known as *C. Madame Octave Opoix*;
C. Princess (*C. Coffinetii* x *C. Fairrieanum*), a handsome hybrid
in which the influence of *C. Fairrieanum* is most marked;
C. Psyche (*C. bellatulum* x *C. niveum*), a hybrid closely akin to the
wild *C. Godefroyæ leucochilum*, and finely represented by its
varieties C. P. Lily and C. P. Mrs H. Druce; C. Redversii
(*C. insigne* x *C. Lucie*), first shown as *C. Sir Redvers Buller*;
C. Reginæ (*C. Fairrieanum* x *C. Leeanum*), a very attractive
*Fairrieanum* cross; C. Richmanii (*C. barbatum* x *C. bellatulum*),
a fine hybrid, first shown as *C. Charles Richman*; C. Rolfei
(*C. bellatulum* x *C. Rothschildeanum*), an interesting and showy

hybrid; C. ROMULUS (*C. insigne* x *C. nitens*), a fine and variable hybrid, its best forms being the varieties C. R. ZENO, C. R. TROILUS, and the handsome C. R. VILLE DE PARIS; C. ROSITA (*C. callosum* x *C. Charlesworthii*).

C. SAVAGEANUM (*C. Harrisianum* x *C. Spicerianum*), a hybrid that has been raised a number of times, and one that is finely represented by such varietal forms as C. S. SEEGERIANUM, C. S. PITCHERIANUM, C. S. ADONIS, C. S. MEMORIA MOENSII, C. S. MADAME CAPPE and C. S. GAETANO; C. SCHLESINGERIANUM (*C. Boxallii* x *C. insigne*), a hybrid of high merit, as represented by the variety C. S. MONS DE CURTE; C. SCHRŒDERI (*C. Fairrieanum* x *C. ænanthum*), is one of the most handsome Cypripediums, and very brightly coloured, but it does not flower freely, the varieties C. S. GERMAINE OPOIX, C. S. GERMAINE OPOIX, WESTFIELD VAR., and C. GASTON BULTEEL, are all superbly coloured, rare and costly; C. STATTERIANUM (*C. Spicerianum* x *C. vexillarium*), richly coloured; C. TAUTZIANUM (*C. barbatum* x *C. niveum*); C. SUPERCILIARE (*C. barbatum* x *C. superbiens*), a good old hybrid; C. VENUS (*C. insigne* x *C. niveum*), a beautiful hybrid, of which the OAKWOOD VARIETY is a fine form; C. VEXILLARIUM (*C. barbatum* x *C. Fairrieanum*), is a charming hybrid, and ought to be grown for its fine form and markings; C. VIPANI (*C. niveum* x *C. philippinense*), is a striking hybrid, and C. V. CORNINGII is a fine variety; C. WOTTONI (*C. bellatulum* x *C. callosum*), is handsome, and in all probability C. PARIS, of uncertain parentage, is a fine varietal form; C. WELLESLEYÆ (*C. Gowerianum* x *C. Sanderianum*), is one of the best hybrids, and one that is fairly well known to specialists under the title of *C. Mrs Francis Wellesley*; C. WELLESLEYI (*C. Lawrenceanum* x *C. Niobe*), is one of Mr Wellesley's fine plants, as also is C. WESTFIELDIENSE (*C. Leeanum* x *C. Pollettianum*).

DENDROBIUM PIERARDII.

In the Phragmopedilum section the following hybrids are good : C. AINSWORTHII (*C. longifolium* x *C. Sedenii*), C. ALBO-PURPUREUM (*C. Dominianum* x C. *Schlimii*), C. CARDINALE (*C. Schlimii* x *C. Sedenii*), C. DOMINIANUM (*C. caricinum* x *C. caudatum*), C. ROSY GEM (*C. cardinale* x *C. Sedenii*), C. SCHRŒDERÆ (*C. caudatum* x *C. Sedenii*), and C. SEDENII (*C. longifolium* x *C. Schlimii*), with its fine variety CANDIDULUM.

## DENDROBIUM

Among the many families of Orchids dealt with in this book, there are few which show such variation in stature, in style of growth, in size and shape of flowers, and in the formation of leafage as do the Dendrobiums. A very large number of the species are mere weeds, and are scarcely worth a second thought except as botanical curiosities, but this still leaves a very large range of choice in form and colour, and were it possible to exclude all the wonderful hybrids from consideration, there would yet be ample material wherewith to brighten our glass-houses for a considerable portion of the year.

When Oloff Swartz, who graduated at the Upsal University, founded the genus in 1800, he described nine species only, but now, rather more than a hundred years later, there are not fewer than four hundred species, in addition to numerous well-marked varieties, and a whole host of hybrids, these latter being themselves often represented by several varieties.

In a wild state Dendrobiums are found distributed over a wide area in the Far East. Among the Nepalese Himalaya they are to be found, but it is, or was, in Burma and in the Moulmein district that the greater number abound. One must write in the past tense with reference to some of them, for there is great difficulty now in finding certain kinds in or near the localities where they were once abundant.   Some species come from the South-west of India, some from Ceylon, and others from Southern China, Cochin China, the Malayan Peninsula, Java, Sumatra, Borneo, and a number from the Philippines, while yet others hail from Timor and New Guinea—notably the lovely and very useful D. *Phalæ-nopsis,* and some from the Western side of Australia and as far South as Tasmania.   This brief reference to the geographical range of a useful family of orchids will at once suggest the need of a whole range of hot-houses, each house kept at a temperature different from the rest, for the proper cultivation of Dendrobiums. But such a need does not exist.   There are a few species that may, without any stretch of imagination, be classed as cool orchids, indeed one at least, *i.e. Dendrobium japonicum,* is occasionally catalogued as hardy.   It may manage to keep alive out-of-doors in exceptionally favoured parts of the South-western counties, but it is never heard of as a real success under out-door treatment. Where a collection rather than a selection is the aim of the grower, then some trouble will be experienced in finding the right condi-tions for the various members of the family.   But where the desire is to have a set of the most beautiful kinds for flowering in the spring and early summer, that desire may be fulfilled provided there is a hot-house (a stove), and a heated vinery at disposal. With such structures, and with the same care and attention paid them as are given to any other indoor crop, there is no good reason why Dendrobiums cannot be successfully managed.

Most of the Dendrobiums worthy of general cultivation are deciduous, but there is a small and important group of evergreen species with showy flowers.   As a general rule Dendrobiums require a very high stove temperature and a moist atmosphere when growing freely, a season of rest in a cooler house and a drier

CATTLEYA  WARSCEW CZII  VAR ETY    THELLO.

atmosphere, and a comfortable intermediate temperature when in flower.    Nearly all of the cultivated Dendrobiums flower in the early spring, following a long resting season.    New growth commences at or about the time of the flowering, usually during March and April, and it is the aim of cultivators to encourage the growth by every possible means, so that it may be completed by the end of the Summer or in early Autumn, while there is sufficient sunshine to make the new stem or pseudo-bulbs firm or ripe before the Winter.    This ripening process is as essential as rapid and vigorous growth, because upon it depends largely the extent and duration of the flower crop the following Spring.    Except when in flower, Dendrobiums require little shading, a thin blind to break up the rays of the sun during the hottest part of a brilliant Summer day being sufficient.    When growth has ceased for the year the plants must be gradually inured to cooler and drier conditions, as their leaves fall, and  they cannot be given too much light from then on to the time of flowering ; and during that period  no water will be needed, unless the pseudo-bulbs show signs of shrivelling.

It is a foolish practice to adhere rigidly to certain degrees of temperature for Dendrobiums  at certain  seasons  of  the  year. Temperature should always be governed by  the  particular condition of the plant or  plants under consideration, together with the prevailing weather.    But for the guidance of the uninitiated it may be broadly stated that in the Winter, when Dendrobiums are at rest, a temperature of not less than 55 degrees should be maintained, rising to 60 or even 65 degrees on  bright  days, but  nothing should be done to excite the plants into premature growth.    In March and April Dendrobiums generally start into growth, and this is the time for re-potting ; the temperature from this period may rise from a minimum of 60 degrees at night to 70 or 75 degrees on bright warm days.    The period of greatest vigour, the

" growing season," as it is technically termed, is during May, June, July and August, and during these months the night temperature ought not to fall below 65 degrees, while, given bright weather and a little ventilation, there is practically no upward limit to the day temperature.    Closing the house early in the afternoon, raising the blinds at the same time, and syringing the plants freely so as to secure strong and moist heat, are points of great importance. When the growth is finished (and " finished " is really a very good technical term, signifying the time when new leaves are no longer produced at the apex of the new pseudo-bulbs), heat and moisture must both be gradually reduced, until, by the end of September, the temperature for March and April is reached ; this may be continued through October, but when the leaves have all fallen, the Winter temperature will suffice.

Although as a class Dendrobiums are of more or less pendulous habit, and therefore well adapted to cultivation in suspended baskets, it is usual to grow them in pots and stake the growths uprightly, as by this means less room is occupied by each specimen.    Whether pots or baskets are used, it is necessary to provide plenty of clean drainage material, and place over this a layer of sphagnum before proceeding further with the potting.    The general potting time is the Spring, when the new growths are advancing and the flowers have faded.    Peat and sphagnum make a suitable compost, and a few broken leaves may be added as the grower comes to understand his plants and the local climatic conditions.    Potting is an easy matter, and consists in placing the compost firmly about the roots after any old and sour material has been removed from the latter. It is quite unnecessary to allow a large number of old pseudo-bulbs to remain ; one, or at most two, of those previously produced will suffice.    Some growers have been eminently successful with *Dendrobium nobile* even when all the old pseudo-bulbs have

DENDROBIUM BRYMERIANUM.

DENDROBIUM CYBELE.

been removed annually, but this drastic treatment is not recommended.

The evergreen species, of which *D. densiflorum* may be taken as the type, like rather more shade than the deciduous kinds when in full growth. Liberal encouragement is desirable as soon as the new growths advance, but the resting season is not so marked in these as in the other species. When at rest the evergreen kinds must be kept in an intermediate house and given sufficient (and only just sufficient) water to keep the leaves and pseudo-bulbs from shrivelling.

There are two marked exceptions to the general rules laid down, and they are D. *Phalænopsis* and D. *formosum giganteum*. The former does not start into new growth until a long time after it has flowered, but as it flowers in the Autumn, this peculiarity does not affect the cultivator so much as at first would appear. D. *formosum giganteum* will not succeed if given the tropical conditions that are suitable for most of the deciduous species, but when placed at the cool end of an intermediate house, it grows and flowers well.

### BEST SPECIES.

D. AUREUM was introduced in 1837; it grows about a foot high, is deciduous, and produces its sweetly fragrant flowers in the Spring. It is one of the first to flower, and when the flower buds are distinctly seen it may be subjected to slight forcing. The flowers, about two and a half inches across, are produced in twos or threes towards the upper part of the stem, and the colour is light cream-yellow, with a deeper yellow lip marked with red-purple. The species has been largely used by the hybridist, and most of the very best hybrids have descended from it.

D. BENSONÆ is a Burmese species, about eighteen inches high,

deciduous, and has stout stems.   The flowers are white, save for
the broad orange stain and two maroon blotches at the base of the
lip.   It blooms freely in the Spring, and is a desirable species.

D. BRYMERIANUM is not an altogether satisfactory plant, as its
flowers are produced sparingly.   But it is worthy of cultivation for
the sake of the few flowers it may produce, as these are among the
most wonderful of the many wonderful flowers seen in Orchids.
The stems are slender, a foot to eighteen inches high, and the
leaves persistent.   The golden yellow flowers are three inches wide,
but the lip is larger than the rest of the flower.   This has prettily
fringed side lobes, and the disk is curiously roughened or papillose,
while the large apical portion broadens out into an exquisitely
beautiful fimbriation, every part branching and rebranching until
the ultimate divisions are of hair-like fineness.   D. BRYMERIANUM
was introduced in 1874 by Messrs Hugh Low & Co., and it is a
Summer flowering species best grown in the Cattleye house or in
an intermediate temperature.

D. CHRYSANTHUM is a very fine species, but as it has stems from
five feet to seven feet long, it occupies considerable space, and therefore is not so popular now that growers prefer a number of small
plants to a few noble specimens.   It is deciduous, Autumn flowering, and produces its deep yellow blooms in racemes on the current
season's growths, while the leaves are still green.   Each flower has
two maroon blotches near the base of the lip.   This species should
be potted directly it has flowered, as new growth commences then;
the Winter temperature ought not to fall below 60 degrees.

D. CRASSINODE is a popular species, found by Col. Benson in
1868.   The thick, semi-pendulous stems are very distinct by reason
of their swollen nodes or joints.   The plants look best when grown
in baskets.   It is a deciduous species and has effective flowers, rather
less than three inches across, white, with deep purple tips to the

sepals, petals and lip, the latter segment having also a broad yellow disk.

D. DEARII is a beautiful Orchid with stout stems two feet or three feet high, and persistent leaves.   The white flowers, each with a yellow-green mark on the lip, appear in late Summer and are produced in racemes, four or five together.   It was found in the Philippine Islands in 1882.

D. DEVONIANUM was found on the Khasia Hills by Gibson, when collecting for the Duke of Devonshire, and was sent to Chatsworth in 1837.   It has slender stems about three feet long, and the flowers appear from the nodes along the greater part of their length.   Though the flowers are not large (about two inches across), they are produced with great freedom, and a large plant in a basket is a fine picture.   The colour is creamy-white, but the petals are purple tinted and the broader petals are tipped with deep magenta-purple, while the lip is blotched with orange at the base and has a purple tip and fringed margins.   A deciduous Spring flowering species.

D. FALCONERI, from Assam, grows from two feet to three feet high, and flowers in Spring.   The flowers are white, all the segments being tipped with purple, while the lip has a purple base and orange markings.   In the variety D. F. ALBIDULUM the white flowers are delicately suffused with pale purple.

D. FARMERI is an evergreen species closely allied to *D. densiflorum*, but the numerous flowers are not so closely set upon the pendulous racemes as in the latter species.   Each flower is about two inches across, straw-yellow, flushed with pink, with a large golden disk on the lip.   It flowers in Spring or early Summer.

D. FIMBRIATUM is a tall grower, its stems often reaching a height of four or five feet. . It is deciduous and carries its flowers in loose pendulous racemes in the Spring.   The rounded flowers are orange-yellow, very pretty and attractive; and the lip is finely fringed. There are several varieties of this North Indian species. The variety D. F. OCULATUM is distinguished by the maroon blotch on the lip.

D. FINDLAYANUM grows about eighteen inches high, is distinctly pendulous, and its swollen nodes give the stems a curiously knotted appearance. It is deciduous, and flowers in Winter or early Spring; its flowers appear from the nodes and they are white, suffused with lilac, the lip being yellow, margined with white.

D. FORMOSUM GIGANTEUM is probably the finest of the white Dendrobiums. The Indian type is so rarely seen and the Moulmein or *giganteum* form so largely imported and cultivated that the varietal name seems quite unnecessary. However, the Orchid so popularly known as D. FORMOSUM GIGANTEUM is a fine one, and as its large white flowers appear in the Autumn it is a valuable plant where choice flowers are in demand at that season. The stems are about fifteen inches high, stout and rigid; the flowers are borne in clusters at the apex of the new leafy growth. D. INFUNDIBULUM and D. JAMESIANUM are closely allied to *D. formosum*, and from a cultivator's point of view they may be considered as less useful varieties of the latter.

D. HILDEBRANDII is a Burmese species that came suddenly into public favour a few years ago. It has twisted sepals and petals, is pale yellow, and flowers very freely.

D. NOBILE is an extremely popular Orchid because it is cheap, easily grown, beautiful, and of great value for many kinds of floral decorations. It appears to have first flowered in this country in Messrs Loddiges' Nursery, at Hackney, in 1837; its introduction was due to Mr J. Russell Reeves, who brought home one plant only. As the species is spread over Northern India, Burmah, and part of China, its introduction in quantity did not occur until the country became opened up somewhat. The species

DENDROBIUM PULCHELLUM.

DENDROBIUM FIMBRIATUM OCULATUM.

is variable in colour, but it usually grows about eighteen inches high, and if not too severely rested its leaves are persistent during the greater part of their second year. The flowers are produced in twos or threes from the nodes along the upper portion of the stems and individually they are about three inches across. The sepals and broader petals are white, with the apical half shading gradually to deep amethyst-purple at the tip; the lip has a deep maroon-purple disk, bordered with cream-white, while there is usually a purple apex. Well marked varieties are D. N. ALBIFLORUM, with flowers that are white except for a dark purple disk; D. N. BALLIANUM, white with a rose-pink disk; D. N. ELEGANS, a fine form with a highly coloured lip; D. N. COOKSONIANUM, a remarkable variety in which the petals are coloured like the lip; D. N. NOBILIUS, a fine variety with all the segments larger and more richly-coloured than any other form known; D. N. SANDERI-ANUM, less brightly coloured than D. N. NOBILIUS and also somewhat smaller; and D. N. VIRGINALE, with lovely white flowers that have a pink disk and a primrose tinted lip.

D. PHALÆNOPSIS is a grand Orchid and one that is deservedly popular. It was not so popular, however, until the introduction of the finer variety from New Guinea, now so well known as D. PHALÆNOPSIS SCHRŒDERIANUM, and it is this that is so largely cultivated for the grace and beauty of its flowers and because it flowers so freely in the Autumn. The varietal form grows about eighteen inches or two feet high and is therefore larger than the type. It carries its large, rounded, Phalænopsis-like flowers in graceful racemes, often as many as twelve or fifteen together, and as they are three to four inches across a few plants in bloom make a fine display. The colour is most variable, but generally rose-purple or magenta-purple, but the range is from pure white in D. P. HOLOLEUCA to the deepest purple.

D. PIERARDII is a very free flowering species, with long, slender, pendulous stems, and if grown well in a basket it is a delightful plant when in bloom in the Spring. The somewhat small flowers, rarely more than two inches across, are pale rose-white, with a primrose coloured lip veined at the base with purple.

D. PRIMULINUM, like the last-named species, is of little value for floral decorations, but it flowers so freely that it deserves to be cultivated for its effectiveness. It has stiff and rather thick stems, about fifteen inches long, semi-pendulous. The chief attraction of the sweetly scented flower is its large rounded, pale yellow, purple-veined lip, the sepals and petals being very narrow in this species, and of a pale rosy lilac shade.

D. PULCHELLUM is a stately and large flowered species, commonly known in gardens as *D. Dalhousieanum*. It is not so free flowering as most of the popular Dendrobiums, and as a consequence it is not so much grown now that the craze is for plants that flower with great freedom and produce flowers that will last a long time when cut. D. PULCHELLUM is a Burmese species introduced in 1837. The stems are three to five feet high, and the flowers are borne in pendulous racemes from the top of the stem. Each flower may measure as much as five inches across, and a raceme may carry as many as ten flowers. The colour is tawny yellow, shaded with rose, the lip having two large maroon-purple blotches at its base.

D. SUPERBIENS is a charming species from North Australia and one that grows about thirty inches high, and flowers in the Autumn. It is allied to *D. Phalænopsis* and carries its crimson-purple flowers in similar fashion.

D. SUPERBUM has pendulous growths, two to three feet long, and its handsome flowers are about four inches across. The latter are curiously Rhubarb-scented, rich rose-purple, with a deep red-

DENDROBIUM THYRSIFLORUM.

purple base to the lip. D. s. ANOSMUM is practically odourless, and smaller than the type, whereas D. s. GIGANTEUM is larger.

D. THYRSIFLORUM is a splendid evergreen species growing about two feet high and flowering in Spring or early Summer. It is very like *D. densiflorum* in habit and carries its white, golden-lipped flowers in considerable numbers on pendulous racemes. It is a very fine plant and for exhibition purposes is quite popular. It comes from Burmah and has been in cultivation since 1864.

D. WARDIANUM runs *D. nobile* closely in point of popularity, and it is in every way a fine Orchid when carrying its large white flowers, every segment tipped with deep amethyst-purple, and the broad lip similarly coloured but with a broad, yellow, maroon blotched base. This species has a fairly wide range through Assam, Burmah, and Indo-China, and for many years it has been imported in large quantities and grown extensively, as its lovely flowers are valuable for bouquets, personal wear, and for other floral purposes. A few flowering plants make a brave show in a warm conservatory in the Spring, and visitors to early flower shows will be quite familiar with the species. The growths vary a good deal and may be from eighteen inches to three feet in length, and though these are distinctly pendulous it is the general custom to stake them upright in cultivation. The growths are stout, with prominent nodes, and the leaves are deciduous. The flowers are often four inches across and are borne in twos or threes along the stems. One fine feature of the flowers of D. WARDIANUM is that their wax-like texture enables them to last a long time in perfection. On the other hand, this species has one great weakness from a cultivator's point of view; it often commences to make new growth late in the season when the growth made in the Spring and early Summer is complete and needs to be ripened,

Cultivators should ignore this new and late attempt to produce growth and proceed along the usual lines of withholding water and resting the plants.    Under these circumstances the late growth is just kept from shrivelling through the Winter, and when the Spring arrives and more genial conditions prevail it will advance rapidly.    The finest forms of D. WARDIANUM come from Burmah and Indo-China, the dwarfer and smaller flowered forms coming from Assam and the Khasia Hills.    The species first flowered in this country in 1858.    There are numerous fine varieties of D. WARDIANUM, differing from the type in form and colouring, but the most distinct variety is D. W. ALBUM, or *D. W. candidum*, apparently identical, with large flowers that are pure white except for the yellow disk.

### BEST HYBRIDS

During the ten years 1890-1900 hybrid Dendrobiums were brought forward in large numbers and raisers were very busy introducing new and beautiful plants of widely diverse parentage.    But more recently the interested amateur has tried his prentice hand on the cool Cypripediums and gone on to be more or less successful with Odontoglossums, and so the hybrids of these genera have become popular in turn and fewer new hybrid Dendrobiums have appeared.    This has one redeeming feature, it has kept the genus from being flooded with a crowd of worthless forms and the majority of the most beautiful hybrids in cultivation are to be purchased at quite reasonable rates.    It is only in the case of extraordinarily fine varieties or a new cross of high merit that the prices rule high.    All are easily cultivated and flower with great freedom.    The following form an excellent selection :—

D. AINSWORTHII (*D. aureum* x *D. nobile*), raised at Manchester in the first instance, first flowered in 1874; it has white sepals and

DENDROBIUM WARDIANUM.

petals and on the lip there is a large and handsome crimson-purple area; it is a fine free-flowering hybrid and one that is well represented in gardens by the type, and by the varietal forms D. A. GRANDIFLORUM, D. A. LEECHIANUM, D. A. ROSEUM, and D. A. SPLENDIDISSIMUM. D. ASPASIA (*D. aureum* x *D. Wardianum*), is a handsome hybrid sometimes known as D. *Wardiano-aureum*. D. CASSIOPE (*D. moniliforme* x *D. nobile*), is a charming and free-flowering plant raised by Mr N. Cookson, and first flowered in 1890; it has white flowers with a maroon-purple blotch on the lip; the white form of *D. nobile* was used as a parent. D. CHESSINGTONENSE (*D. aureum* x *D. Wiganiæ*), is one of the newer hybrids raised by Mr Thwaites, and flowered in 1905; it is a strong grower and has soft yellow flowers with a deep brown blotch on the lip. D. COOKSONI (*D. nobile* x *D. Wiganiæ*), appeared in 1904, and combines the good features of its parents. D. CURTISII (*D. aureum* x *D. Cassiope*), is an unusually free flowering hybrid raised by Messrs Sander & Sons, and named in compliment to the writer. D. CYBELE (*D. Findlayanum* x *D. nobile*), is best represented by the OAKWOOD VARIETY, in which the yellow seen in the lip of D. *Findlayanum* is well brought out. D. ELLISII (*D. Hildebrandii* x D. *nobile*), is a strong grower, and has yellowish flowers; D. WIGANIANUM must be regarded as a variety of this hybrid. D. EUOSMUM (*D. endocharis* x *D. nobile*), an old hybrid, raised by Seden, and flowered in 1885, has white flowers tipped with purple, and with a rose-purple disc, and it is fragrant. D. GEM (*D. aureum* x *D. Ainsworthii*), is a fine hybrid with a creamy yellow suffusion; D. ARTEMIS is of the same parentage. D. ILLUSTRE (*D. chrysotoxum* x *D. pulchellum*), is a pretty and interesting cross. D. LUTWYCHEANUM (*D. Ainsworthii* x *D. Wardianum*), is a splendid hybrid from two splendid parents, and it is fairly well known as D. CLIO, but the latter, as well as D. L. SUPERBUM and D. L. TYNTESFIELD VAR., must be considered as fine varietal forms of the same cross.

D. MELANODISCUS (*D. Ainsworthii* × D. *Findlayanum*), raised in Sir Trevor Lawrence's collection, is an extremely variable hybrid, but all the varieties that have received names are beautiful; D. CHRYSODISCUS is the reverse cross, and has more yellow in the lip than the original D. MELANODISCUS; D. M. GLORIOSUM, D. M. CLYTIE, D. M. DIDO, D. M. HEBE, D. M. LUNA, D. M. PALLENS, and D. M. RAINBOW are all charming, and indicate the great variation to be obtained from a hybrid when each parent is used both as a pollen and seed parent. D. MELPOMENE (*D. Ainsworthii* × *D. signatum*), is a first-rate hybrid. D. MICANS (*D. lituiflorum* × *D. Wardianum*), is a Veitchian hybrid that first flowered in 1879, but is still worthy of cultivation, and is mostly found in gardens now under the names of D. ALCIPPE and D. EURYCLEA, these representing the reverse cross. D. MURRHINIACUM (*D. nobile* × *D. Wardianum*), is a handsome hybrid between the two most popular species, and it is also known as *D. Euterpe*, *D. nobile-Wardianum*, and *D. Wardiano-nobile*. D. OPHIR (*D. aureum* × *D. signatum*), is yellow flowered. D. RUBENS (*D. Ainsworthii* × *D. nobile*), is one of the very best of artificially raised Dendrobiums, and has been obtained by crossing the parents both ways; it has been raised many times, and there are a number of interesting and beautiful varietal forms, notably D. R. APOLLO, D. R. DELLENSE, D. R. EURYALUS, D. R. GRANDIFLORUM, D. R. HECTOR, D. R. OTHELLO, and D. R. VIRGIL. D. SCHNEIDERIANUM (*D. aureum* × *D. Findlayanum*), is a showy hybrid with a great deal of yellow colouring. D. THWAITESIÆ (*D. Ainsworthii* × *D. Wiganiæ*), is a bright and beautiful hybrid of yellow hue. D. VENUS (*D. Falconeri* × *D. nobile*), is a very fine hybrid, in which the purple colour and the yellow disc are very marked. D. WALTONI (*D.*

DENDROBIUM FORMOSUM GIGANTEUM.

*crassinode* x *D. Wardianum*), appeared naturally, and has been also raised artificially.    D. WIGANIÆ (*D. nobile* x *D. signatum*), is another of the fine series of modern hybrids with yellow colouring; it has been raised several times, and has a distinct variety in D. W. XANTHOCHEILUM.

### OTHER SPECIES AND HYBRIDS

Among species that are deserving of attention where there is room for more than those already noted, the following may be selected :—D. ATROVIOLACEUM, a species from New Guinea, with violet lip; D. BARBATULUM, white flowers in close racemes; D. BIGIBBUM, an Australian species with rounded, deep purple flowers; D. CHRYSOTOXUM, a Burmese species with yellow flowers, short, thick, pseudo-bulbs, and long leathery leaves ; D. CŒLOGYNE, a striking species with large Cœlogyne-like flowers, coloured green and purple; D. CRETACEUM, flowers dull white, with yellow, red-marked lip; D. CRYSTALLINUM, white, tipped with purple, very free flowering; D. HARVEYANUM, bright yellow, with fimbriated petals; D. LINAWIANUM, a rather rare species with rose-purple flowers; D. LOWII, about a foot high, flowers light buff-yellow; D. MACCARTHIÆ, a curious species that has large, flattened flowers, rosy mauve and rich purple; D. MOSCHATUM, yellow, with dark maroon base to the lip, musk scented; D. OCHREATUM. a dwarf plant with orange-yellow flowers; D. SANGUINOLENTUM, amber-yellow with red-purple markings; D. SPECIOSUM, an Australian species that does not need the tropical conditions afforded most Dendrobiums : the flowers are small, buff coloured, sweetly scented, and carried in stiff, dense racemes : the variety HILLII has whiter flowers dotted with purple, and makes a fine specimen when well managed ; D. VICTORIA-REGINA, the so-called " blue " Dendrobium from the Philippine Islands, has small, bluish purple flowers: it does not flower very freely, but is quite distinct and novel.

A further selection from the hybrid Dendrobiums should include — D. BLACKIANUM (*D. Findlayanum* × *D. Wiganiæ*), D. BOUNDII (*D. Findlayanum* × D. *Hildebrandii*), D. BRYAN (D. *luteolum* × *D. Wardianum*), D. CHELTENHAMENSE (*D. aureum* × *D. luteolum*), D. CORDELIA (D. *aureum* × *D. euosmum*), D. CYPHERII (*D. crassinode* × *D. Findlayanum*), D. DOMINYANUM (*D. Linawianum* × *D. nobile*), D. DORIS (D. *Ainsworthii* × D. *moniliforme*), D. GATTONENSE (D. *Curtisii* × D. *Findlayanum*), D. NIOBE (D. *nobile* × D. *tortile*), D. PITCHERIANUM (D. *nobile* × D. *primulinum*), known also as D. *Rolfeæ*; D. SCYLLA (D. *Cybele* × D. *moniliforme*), and D. THOMPSONIANUM (D. *Cheltenhamense* × D. *nobile*).


## DISA

To amateurs who do not care to provide and maintain accommodation for tropical Orchids, the genus Disa offers a fine opportunity. Everyone who knows the Disas agrees that they are beautiful, elegant, useful, and easily grown, and yet there are very few indeed who take up their cultivation seriously and make them the success they deserve to be. The hybrids, and all the species except D. *grandiflora*, are finely grown at Kew, where several hybrids have been raised. D. *grandiflora* flowers at Kew, but is not the striking success there that it has been at Joldwynds, Dorking, or at Messrs Cripps & Son's nurseries at Tunbridge Wells; indeed this, the finest member of the family, is flowered in first-rate style in but few gardens, owing probably to insufficiently moist and cool atmospheric conditions during the growing season.

The Disas are terrestrial, and chiefly from South Africa;

DISA GRANDIFLORA.

most of them have tuberous roots, and a rosette-like cluster of green leaves, from which in due course arises a leafy flower spike, carrying several flowers, each flower with conspicuous sepals. D. GRANDIFLORA has broad, scarlet sepals, and its flowers, four or five inches across, are borne in early Summer or Autumn, several together on a stem upwards of twenty inches high. D. RACEMOSA has numerous small rose-purple flowers on stems eighteen inches high. D. TRIPETALOIDES has small, pretty, white, pink-shaded flowers, lightly spotted with red.

The chief hybrids are D. KEWENSIS (D. *grandiflora* x D. *tripetaloides*), raised at Kew; D. LANGLEYENSIS (D. *racemosa* x D. *tripetaloides*), raised by the Messrs Veitch; D. LUNA (*D. racemosa* x *D. Veitchii*), also raised by the Messrs Veitch; D. PREMIER (D. *tripetaloides* x D. *Veitchii*), with deep rose-coloured flowers, one of the best. D. VEITCHII (D. *grandiflora* x D. *racemosa*), bright rose-purple, very fine, and ranking next to D. *grandiflora* in point of merit, with D. PREMIER and D. KEWENSIS following closely.

Disas are best grown in shallow pans, in a compost of fibrous peat, sphagnum, and sand, placed over ample drainage. The time for potting is when new roots are being made. Moisture at the roots and in the atmosphere must be always provided, as drought is certain to bring failure and will probably kill the plants, but excessive watering after the flowering season is over must be avoided, as the plants then enjoy a season of comparative rest, and the syringe rather than the watering-can should be used. The coolest end of the Odontoglossum House will often provide a suitable position for Disas all through the dull months of the year and until flowering is over, but for the rest of the year a frame in a sheltered and shady position, with an abundance of moisture holding material (ashes or shingle, or even a bed of sphagnum moss), will be found suitable. Shade, moisture, and plenty of fresh air are very necessary to the well-being of Disas, and if pains are taken to provide these, the grower will be rewarded with beautiful flowers, and will come fully to understand why *D. grandiflora*, the gem of the Table Mountain, is popularly called "The Flower of the Gods."

## EPIDENDRUM

Although the genus Epidendrum is a very large one in point of numbers, it is by no means one of the most useful from a cultivator's point of view. Considering the many species it contains (over four hundred), it has few of first-rate importance for garden purposes. As Epidendrums are distributed over a very wide area in South America, it might be expected that under cultivation they require varied conditions, but this is not so, for with the exception of the lovely little *E. vitellinum majus*, all may be managed very well in an intermediate house. Those with pseudo-bulbs well defined are best grown with the Cattleyas and Lælias, but those with slender, flexuous stems need moist atmospheric conditions the whole year through, but a diminished supply of water at the roots when resting. Peat and sphagnum provide a suitable rooting medium, and potting should be done as new roots appear. The taller, slender-stemmed kinds should be freely syringed when in full growth. All Epidendrums are evergreen.

### Best Species and Hybrids

E. CINNABARINUM grows four feet high, and its slender stems are crowned in Spring or early Summer with terminal clusters of scarlet, orange-lipped flowers. E. EVECTUM is a tall, leafy-stemmed species, and one that is almost always in flower, bearing long-

DENDROBIUM AUREUM.

stemmed spikes of rich rose-purple blooms of moderate size. E. PRISMATOCARPUM is a fine plant for exhibition purposes, and is frequently seen at exhibitions in late Spring and early Summer; its pseudo-bulbs are crowned with a pair of stout, leathery leaves, and from the top of each pseudo-bulb an erect spike is produced; the cream-coloured flowers are spotted with dark purple, and the lip is yellow and rose.    E. RADICANS grows upwards of two feet high, and as it produces ærial roots freely, propagation is easily effected by removing a portion of the growth with roots attached; it does not bloom so freely as E. CINNABARINUM, but its large terminal clusters of brilliant orange-scarlet flowers are very beautiful.    E. VITELLINUM is not much grown, but E. VITELLINUM MAJUS, which has larger flowers, is practically indispensable in an Orchid collection, and of great value in any establishment where choice flowers for bouquets and other floral arrangements are required; it is a lowly plant, seldom exceeding a foot in height; the pseudo-bulbs are small and rounded, and carry a pair of ovate, glaucous-green leaves, which are surmounted in the Summer by a sturdy spike of flowers, each an inch or a little more broad, and of the most vivid cinnabar-orange colour imaginable.    E. VITELLINUM MAJUS should be grown with the Odontoglossums.    E. WALLISII is almost a continuous bloomer; it has dark, slender stems, upwards of two feet high, these bearing several flowers near the apex.    The flowers of E. WALLISII are among the largest seen in the genus, and are often two inches across; they are yellow, marked with crimson, while the white lip has red-purple markings.

A number of good hybrids have been raised, and the best of these are—E. BOUNDII (*E. Burtoni* x *E. radicans*), deep orange-scarlet; E. BURTONI (*E. ibaguense* x *E. O'Brienianum*), very free flowering, rosy crimson to crimson-scarlet; E. CASSIOPE (*E. radicans* x *E. vitellinum*), orange-yellow; E. CLARISSA (*E. elegan-*

*tulum* x *Wallisii*), somewhat like, but finer than, *E. Wallisii*, and first exhibited as *E. Wallisii-elegantulum* ; E. DELLENSE (*E. radicans* × *E. xanthinum*), orange-vermilion, flowers in large clusters ; E. ELEGANTULUM (*E. Veitchii* x *E. Wallisii*), yellow or yellowish brown, with red-purple markings ; E. O'BRIENIANUM (*E. evectum* x *E. radicans*), bright carmine, with orange mark on the lip ; E. VEITCHII (*E. Endresii* x *E. Wallisii*), better known at present in gardens as *E. Endresio-Wallisii*, heavily suffused and marked with purple on a yellowish ground.

### OTHER SPECIES AND HYBRIDS

A few more of the species that have some claim to general cultivation are E. ATROPURPUREUM and its variety E. A. RANDII ; E. CILIARE, with fringed white lip ; E. COCHLEATUM, E. COOPERI ANUM, E. ENDRESII, E. FRAGRANS, an old sweetly scented kind ; E. FREDERICI-GUILIELMI, E. MEDUSÆ (better known as *Nanodes Medusæ*), a very interesting, low growing species, with dull purple flowers ; E. PARKINSONIANUM, E. STAMFORDIANUM, E. VARIE-GATUM, and E. VERRUCOSUM.

Other interesting hybrids besides those already enumerated are E. CHARLESWORTHII (*E. Frederici-Guilielmi* x *E. radicans*), E. GATTONENSE (*E. Boundii* × *E. xanthinum*), E. HEATONENSE (*E. Cooperianum* x *E. O'Brienianum*), E. KEWENSE (*E. evectum* x *E. xanthinum*), E. ORPETI (*E. elongatum* x *E. O'Brienianum*), and E. SEDENI (*E. ciliare* × *E. Wallisii*).

## EPIPHRONITIS

At the time of writing only two hybrids between a Sophron-itis and an Epidendrum have been recorded. The first of these is EPIPHRONITIS VEITCHII, a delightful little plant that grows about a foot high, and yields an abundance of brilliant crimson-scarlet

EPIDENDRUM  VITELLINUM  MAJUS.

flowers, like broad, flattened Epidendrums, each with a prominent yellow blotch on the lip. It grows with the utmost freedom at the cool end of the intermediate house, and can be propagated by division with great ease. The parents are *Sophronitis grandiflora* and *Epidendrum radicans*. The second hybrid is EPIPHRONITIS ORPETI, of American origin, and derived from *Epidendrum O'Brienianum* and *Sophronitis violacea*.

## LÆLIA

The Lælias are a fairly large family of, for the most part, very effective, beautiful, and useful Orchids. In some instances it is difficult to distinguish a Lælia from a Cattleya in outward appearance, but as a rule the Lælias have not such large flowers as Cattleyas, and the flowers have narrower segments. Botanically the difference is also very slight, and consists in the Lælias having eight pollinia instead of four as in Cattleya. Lælias intercross readily with Cattleyas, and the hybrids, known as Lælio-Cattleyas, form a splendid group of very beautiful plants. The two families are found in Brazil, Mexico, and Guatemala, and with the exception of the Mexican group the Lælias thrive under the conditions found most suitable for the majority of Cattleyas.

The Mexican Lælias form a group differing in habit and requirements from the rest of the family. Most of these have thick, short, compressed pseudo-bulbs, and long, slender spikes bearing the flowers near the apex.

### BEST SPECIES

L. ANCEPS is a beautiful winter-flowering Mexican species first introduced in 1835 by the Messrs Loddiges of Hackney. It is very variable in the colour of its flowers, but in every case the spikes are from two to three feet long, and carry from two to five flowers near the apex.    Each flower is about four inches across, with spreading and almost equal sepals and petals, and a three-lobed lip, the side lobes being enfolded over the column, and the front lobe extended and slightly reflexed.    In the type the flowers are rose-purple, with a lip of deeper shade, the edges of the side lobes and the whole of the front lobe being deep crimson-purple. The disk is yellow, bordered with white.    The principal varieties are L. A. ALBA, white, with a yellow throat; L. A. AMESIÆ, deep purple with crimson shading; L. A. BALLANTINEANA, rich rose-purple, with crimson lines in the yellow throat; L. A. DAWSONII, white, with purple marks on the lip, very fine; L. A. HILLII, white, with a pink lip, and yellow, crimson-marked throat; L. A. SANDERIANA, white, with rose-purple blotch on the front lobe of the lip; L. A. SCHRŒDERÆ, deep purple, large, and of fine form, lip crimson-purple; L. A. SCHRŒDERIANA, a strong grower, white, with crimson marks in the throat; L. A. STELLA, white, with a few rosy lines in the yellow throat; L. A. VESTALIS, white, with purple lines in the throat; L. A. WILLIAMSIANA, white, throat deep orange-yellow, lined with crimson; L. A. VEITCHII, white, with the lip marked with rose-purple.

L. AUTUMNALIS is another Mexican species, somewhat like and only a little less valuable than *L. anceps*.    It is similar in habit, and carries six or more flowers towards the end of the long spike.    The flowers are from three to four inches across, fragrant, and with a more open lip than in *L. anceps*.    The colour is deep rose-purple, with a white base to the lip and a yellow crest.    In L. A. ALBA the flowers are white, with some yellow in the throat; while in L. A. ATRORUBENS the colour is deeper and richer than in the type.

L. CINNABARINA, about nine inches high, has slender pseudo-

DENDROBIUM PHALAENOPSIS SCHRŒDERIANUM (LIGHT VARIETY).

bulbs and an erect spike of from six to fifteen bright cinnabar-red flowers. Each flower is about two inches and a half across, the sepals and petals are narrow, and the lip is marked with red. A very attractive and useful species that blooms in the Spring.

L. DAYANA is very like *L. pumila* in general appearance, and is frequently referred to as a variety of the latter species. It has short pseudo-bulbs, each carrying one thick green leaf. The flowers are rounded, about four inches across, rose-purple, with a white base to the lip. It is a pretty orchid, dwarf, showy, and best grown in a suspended pan or basket.

L. FLAVA is a Brazilian species with tapering pseudo-bulbs about six inches high, and erect spike a foot or more long, carrying from four to nine flowers. The colour in soft orange-yellow.

L. GRANDIS is of Cattleya-like habit, about eighteen inches high, and it carries its flowers, three to five together, in a short, stiff spike. Each flower is five or six inches across, nankeen yellow, with a rose-purple lip veined with white.

L. JONGHEANA, now that it has been imported in quantity, is a popular species, and deservedly so, as it is of dwarf habit and bears large showy flowers. It is about six inches high, and though two or three flowers are usually produced from one spike, as many as five have been noted on an imported spike. The segments are broad and the whole flower flattened, five or six inches across, bright rose-purple, with a yellow disc on the lip. The flowering time is Winter and Spring.

L. PERRINII is a fine old species introduced more than seventy years ago, but now seldom grown. Its pseudo-bulbs are from six to nine inches long, and the leaves are of similar length. The flowers are five inches across, flat, pale rose-purple, with a deep purple apex to the lip. The variety L. P. NIVEA is white with a purple apex to the lip and a light yellow throat.

L. PUMILA is a variable species, especially if we regard L. DAYANA and L. PRÆSTANS as varieties. L. DAYANA, given specific rank at Kew, may be considered for horticultural purposes as a strong, deeper-coloured form of L. PUMILA, while L. PRÆSTANS differs in having a trumpet-shaped lip, red-purple with yellow shading in the throat. L. PUMILA does not exceed six inches in height and has handsome rose-purple flowers. All three members of this little group are very suitable for amateurs with limited accommodation, as they grow best in suspended pans or baskets and take up little space.

L. PURPURATA is the finest member of the family, and when not in flower has much the appearance of some of the labiate Cattleyas, and it succeeds well with these. Well-developed flowers of a good form have a spread of eight inches, but they lack the breadth of petal found in the popular Cattleyas. From three to nine flowers are borne on a stout spike in Spring or early Summer. In the type the sepals and petals are white, flushed with rose, the large lip being of similar shade, with crimson lines in the pale yellow throat, and a broad red-purple front lobe. There are numerous varieties, and a few of the finest of these are L. P. ALBA, L. P. ATROPURPUREA, L. P. BRYSIANA, L. P. RUSSELLIANA, and L. P. SCHRŒDERIANA.

L. TENEBROSA is very like L. purpurata in growth, but its flowers have rather broader petals and the lip is more trumpet-shaped. The colour is reddish brown, with coppery or bronze suffusion, the lip purple, with darker shading and lighter veinings. L. TENEBROSA is variable in its colouring, and is closely allied to L. grandis. L. T. CHARLESWORTHII, L. T. TRING PARK VAR., L. T. WALTON GRANGE VAR. (yellow sepals and petals), and L. T. WARNHAM COURT VAR., are among the best forms.

VARIETIES OF LÆLIA ANCEPS.

## BEST HYBRIDS

The Lælia hybrids are not so numerous as the Lælio-Cattleyas, nor are they, as a class, so generally useful as the latter. There are, however, a few of considerable beauty, and among these the best are:—L. BRESEIS (*L. harpophylla* x *L. purpurata*), L. CINNA-BROSA (*L. cinnabarina* x *L. tenebrosa*), L. DAPHNE (*L. Dayana* x *L. purpurata*), L. EDISSA (*L. anceps* x *L. purpurata*), L. EUTERPE (*L. crispa* x *L. Dayana*), L. GRAVESIÆ (*L. crispa* x *L. pumila*), L. IONA (*L. Dayana* x *L. tenebrosa*), L. LATONA (*L. cinnabarina* x *L. tenebrosa*), L. LAWRENCEI (*L. grandiflora* x *L. purpurata*), L. NIGRESCENS (*L. pumila* x *L. tenebrosa*), L. OWENIANA (*L. Dayana* x *L. xanthina*), L. PULCHERRIMA (*L. Boothiana* x *L. purpurata*), and L. STANISLAUS (*L. autumnalis* x *L. cinnabarina*).

## OTHER SPECIES AND HYBRIDS

All the following have some special attraction, and are worthy of cultivation where space permits. L. ALBIDA, a white, rose-tinted, Mexican species; L. BOOTHIANA, large purple flowers; *L. crispa*, white flowers with crisped purple lip; L. CRISPILABIA, small rosy lilac flowers; L. CRAWSHAYANA, a supposed natural hybrid between *L. albida* and *L. anceps*, purple; L. EYERMANIANA, a Mexican species with rosy purple flowers; L. FURFURACEA, a Mexican species, somewhat like *L. autumnalis*; L. GOULDIANA, a rare Mexican plant, and supposed to be a natural hybrid between *L. anceps* and *L. autumnalis*; L. GRANDIFLORA, a Summer flowering species with rosy lilac and white flowers; L. HARPOPHYLLA, a slender Winter-flowering species with orange-coloured flowers; L. MONOPHYLLA, a low-growing species from Jamaica, bearing small bright orange-scarlet flowers; L. RUBESCENS, a white Winter-flowering Mexican species; L. SUPERBIENS, a fine species when well grown, but its rosy flowers do not last long; it has tall spikes, three to five feet high, carrying from six to twenty flowers of good size; and L. XANTHINA, a yellow-flowered species that blooms in early Summer.

A few more important hybrids are :—L. AMŒNA (*L. anceps* x *L. pumila*), L. DIONA (*L. Dayana* x *L. purpurata*), L. DEGEES-TIANA (*L. flava* x *L. Jongheana*), L. EXQUISITE (*L. Dayana* x *L. Perrinii*), L. FLAMMEA (*L. cinnabarina* x *L. Pilcheri*), L. CLAVINA (*L. flava* x *L. pumila*), L. GWENNIE (*L. Cowanii* x *L. Jongheana*), L. ICARIUS (*L. cinnabarina* x *L. flava*), L. JUVENILIS (*L. Perrinii* x *L. pumila*), L. MARONI (*L. acuminata* x *L. anceps*), L. MAN-TINII (*L. grandis* x *L. purpurata*), L. MINERVA (*L. Latona* x *L. tenebrosa*), L. MOZART (*L. Boothiana* x *L. tenebrosa*), L. NEMESIS (*L. anceps* x *L. superbiens*), L. SPLENDENS (*L. crispa* x *L. pur-purata*), and L. STELLATA (*L. harpophylla* x *L. tenebrosa*).


## LÆLIO-CATTLEYA

Should a doubt linger in the mind of anyone as to the value of hybrid Orchids, or the place these are already taking in the floricultural world, such doubt would soon be dispelled if the doubter were to visit the regular meetings of the leading horti-cultural societies of England, France, Belgium and America, for at no season of the year is a display of Orchids now made without one or more Lælio-Cattleyas appearing.

Culturally, these hybrids need the same treatment as the majority of Cattleyas, but where one of the more or less " difficult " Lælias or Cattleyas has been used as a parent, some consideration must be given to the particular likings of such species.

Any selection of Lælio-Cattleyas must necessarily be open to

ODONTOGLOSSUM CRISPUM (SPOTTED VARIETY).

criticism, simply because the range of habit and the size and colour of the flowers is so wonderfully wide that there is room for a great divergence of taste. Moreover, what is best to–day may not be the best to-morrow. At almost every meeting of the London and Manchester Orchid Committees some new hybrid or new variety of a previously raised hybrid appears, and though the standard of judgment is being continually raised, Certificates and Awards of Merit are frequently granted. The eighteen here selected as " the best" include a wide range of colouring, and as many of them have been in cultivation for several years, their value has been fully demonstrated.

### Best Hybrids

L.-C. Aphrodite (*C. Mendelii* x *L. purpurata*), is a fine Orchid, and L.-C. A. Eudora, L.-C. A. King Edward VII., and L.-C. A. Ruth are splendid forms; L.-C. Bletchleyensis (*C. Warscewiczii* x *L. tenebrosa*); L.-C. callistoglossa (*C. Warscewiczii* x *L. purpurata*), is very beautiful and variable; L.-C. Canhamiana (*C. Mossiæ* x *L. purpurata*), is one of the older hybrids, and its finer forms are L.-C. C. alba, L.-C. C. excelsa, L.-C. C. Lady Wigan, and L.-C. C. Princess of Wales; L.-C. Charlesworthii (*C. Dowiana* x *L. cinnabarina*), is a brilliant and beautiful winter-flowering hybrid; L.-C. elegans is a fine natural hybrid between *C. Leopoldi* and *L. purpurata*; L.-C. Ernesti (*C. Percivaliana* x *L. flava*); L.-C. Euphrosyne (*C. Warscewiczii* x *L. Dayana*); L.-C. exoniensis (*C .Mossiæ* x *L. crispa*); L.-C. Fascinator (*C. Schrœderæ* x *L. purpurata*), a remarkably beautiful and variable Spring-flowering hybrid; L.-C. Fournieræ (*C. Dowiana* x *L.-c. elegans*), better known as *L.-c. Berthe Fournier*; L.-C. Greenwoodii (*C. Hardyana* x *L.-c. Schilleriana*), better known as *L.-c. Henry Greenwood*; L.-C. Golden Oriole

(*C. Dowiana* x *L.-c. Charlesworthii*), bright golden yellow; L.-c. HIPPOLYTA (*C. Mossiæ* × *L. cinnabarina*); L.-c. INGRAMI (*C. Dowiana* × *L. Dayana*); L.-c. MARTINETTII (*C. Mossiæ* × *L. tenebrosa*); L.c.-SCHILLERIANA (*C. intermedia* x *L. purpurata*), a variable natural hybrid, also raised artificially, somewhat like *L.-c. elegans*; L.-c. TRUFFAUTIANA (*C. Dowiana* x *L. tenebrosa*), a handsome hybrid, also well known as *L.-c. Luminosa*, and finely represented by its varieties L.-c. T. FOURNIERII and L.-c. T. THE MIKADO.

### OTHER HYBRIDS

A further selection includes: L.-c. ALEXANDERI (*C. granulosa* × *L.-c. elegans*), L.-c. ANDROMEDA (*C. Dowiana* x *L. flava*), L.-c. ANTIGONE (*C. Schilleriana* x *L. purpurata*), L.-c. ASCANIA (*C. Trianæ* × *L. xanthina*), L.-c. ASTORIÆ (*C. Gaskelliana* × *L. xanthina*), also known as *L.-c. Hon. Mrs Astor* and *L.-c. Yellow Prince*; L.-c. BADEN POWELLII (*C. Lawrenceana* × *L. tenebrosa*), L.-c. BALLII (*C. Schræderæ* × *L. cinnabarina*), L.-c. BELLA (*C. labiata* x *L. purpurata*), L.-c. BOYLEI (*C. Trianæ* × *L. anceps*), L.-c. BRYAN (*C. Gaskelliana* × *L. crispa*), L.-c. CAPPEI (*C. Warscewiczii* × *L. cinnabarina*), L.-c. CHOLETIANA (*C. Mossiæ* × *L. superbiens*), a very interesting, beautiful, and free-flowering hybrid, with most likeness to the Lælia parent; L.-c. CLIVE (*C. Dowiana* × *L. pumila*), L.-c. CLONIA (*C. Warscewiczii* × *L.-c. elegans*), L.c. DARWINIANA (*C. maxima* × *L.-c. elegans*), L.-c. DECIA (*C. Dowiana* x *C. Perrinii*), L.-c. DEVONIENSIS (*C. Leopoldi* x *L. crispa*), L.-c. DEWEYI (*C. Warneri* × *L.-c. elegans*), L.-c. DOMINIANA (*C. Dowiana* × *L. purpurata*), L.-c. DORA (*C. Schræderæ* × *L.-c. Hippolyta*), L.-c. DORIS (*C. Trianæ* × *L. harpophylla*), L.-c. EPICASTA (*C. Warscewiczii* × *L. pumila*), L.-c. EVA (*C. Gaskelliana* × *L. tenebrosa*), L.-c.

LÆLIO-CATTLEYA SYLVIA.

FORTUNA (*C. Mossiæ* x *L.-c. Schilleriana*), L.-C. GOTTOIANA (*C. Warneri* x *L. tenebrosa*), L.-C. GOLDEN BELLE (*C. Dowiana* x *L.-c. Ernesti*), L.-C. GOLDEN GLORY (*C. Mossiæ* x *L.-c. Zephyra*), L.-C. HAROLDIANA (*C. Hardyana* x *L. tenebrosa*), L.-C. HELENA (*C. Schilleriana* x *L. cinnabarina*), L.-C. HYEANA (*C. Lawrenceana* x *L. purpurata*), L.-C. KING MANOEL, brilliant orange-red, parentage unrecorded; L.-C. LUSTRE (*C. Lueddemanniana* x *L.-c. callistoglossa*), L.-C. MYRA (*C. Triana* x *L. flava*), L.-C. PALLAS (*C. Dowiana* x *L. crispa*), L.-C. ROTHSCHILDIÆ (*C. Warscewiczii* x *L. Perrinii*), L.-C. SCHRŒDERÆ (*C. Trianæ* x *L. Jongheana*), L.-C. SYLVIA (*L.-c. Hippolyta var.* x *L.-c. Ascania*), L.-C. VEITCHIANA (*C. labiata* x *L. crispa*), L.-C. WARNHAMENSIS (*C. Trianæ* x *L. cinnabarina*), L.-C. WELLSIANA (*C. Trianæ* x *L. purpurata*), L.-C. WIGANIÆ (*C. Mossiæ* x *L.-c. Gottoiana*), L.-C. ZENOBIA (*C. Loddigesii* x *L.-c. elegans*), and L.-C. ZEPHYRA (*C. Mendelii* x *L. xanthina*).

## LYCASTE

Among the half-dozen Orchids that an amateur who has some knowledge of horticulture may presume to cultivate with reasonable success, even with fairly limited means and accommodation, *Lycaste Skinneri* must take a place. This species raises the genus to a place of importance among Orchids and quite redeems it from mediocrity. Even granted that some of the Lycastes are beautiful, Dr Lindley's name for the genus suggests greater beauty and elegance than the genus possesses, for was not Lycaste the beautiful daughter of Priam?

Lycastes come from Tropical America, and have short, thick pseudo-bulbs, and large, plaited leaves. As a general rule, the flowers are carried singly on stout, erect stems that proceed from the base of the last-made pseudo-bulb.   The flowers are of good size, often four or five inches across, fleshy, and of stiff appearance, but they are effective and last a long time, four or five weeks, in good condition.   Lycastes may be grown successfully at the cool end of the intermediate house or with the Odontoglossums, but if the cooler conditions are provided then every care must be taken to avoid over-watering, especially during the resting period, or the plants will suffer.

Many amateurs grow *Lycaste Skinneri* in an ordinary warm greenhouse, without any artificial heat whatever during the Summer months.   Fibrous peat and a little chopped sphagnum suit the various species, but as a cultivator gains confidence and experience a mixture of fibrous peat, fibrous loam, broken leaves, and sand may be substituted as a rooting medium, provided the water-pot is used with great discretion.   In the Winter, and when the plants are resting and almost or entirely leafless, very little water will suffice.   Potting is best done as soon as the new growths have advanced an inch or two and new roots have begun to form.

### Best Species and Hybrids

L. aromatica has golden yellow flowers, about three inches across, fragrant, and several may be produced from the base of one bulb, in the Summer.   The flower stems are about four inches high.

L. Deppei, a Mexican species, is rather larger than *L. aromatica*, and the flowers are set on longer stems.   The sepals are green, marked with purple-brown, petals white, and the lip yellow, dotted with crimson.   Spring and early Summer is the usual flowering season.

L. macrophylla (identical with *L. plana*), is a strong-growing

LYCASTE SKINNERI (LIGHT VARIETY).

species from Peru; the olive green sepals are shaded with red-brown, and the petals are white with rosy spots, while the lip is also rose and white, with crimson spots. The variety L. M. MEASURE-SIANA has browner sepals, and the rest of the flower is more deeply and densely spotted than the type.

L. SKINNERI is a very variable species in the matter of colour, and where a large batch of this useful Orchid is grown the flowering period may extend from November to March or April. The usual colour is a pale shade of rose, the lip being whitish, with deep crimson spots and shading. The sepals spread out stiffly, and the smaller petals and the lip point forward, making a central feature round the column. Some varieties are deep rose-purple or intense mauve, while at the other end of the scale is the pure white L. S. ALBA. L. S. ARMENIACA, buff tinted; L. S. HELLEMENSE, very finely coloured; L. S. ROSEA, deep rose, with white lip; and L. S. VIRGINALIS, white, flushed with silvery rose, are the foremost varieties.

The finest hybrid is undoubtedly L. BALLIÆ, from *L. macrophylla* and *L. Skinneri*. L. CAPPEI, L. CHARLESWORTHII, and L. MARY GRATRIX are from the same cross, and therefore varietal forms of the same hybrid.

### OTHER SPECIES AND HYBRIDS

L. BARRINGTONIÆ, greenish yellow; L. BREVISPATHA, green, white, and rose-purple; L. CRUENTA, yellow; L. GIGANTEA, green and purple; L. LANIPES, white and green; L. MACROBULBON, yellow and orange; L. SCHILLERIANA, creamy white; and L. TETRAGONA, yellow-green, brown, and violet, are all good species.

Other hybrids are L. GROGANII (*L. aromatica* x *L. Deppei*);

H

L. HYBRIDA (*L. Deppei* × *L. Skinneri*), L. IMSCHOOTIANA (*L. cruenta* × *L. Skinneri*); L. JANETIÆ (*L. Rossiana* × *L. Skinneri*), and L. SCHŒNBRUNNENSIS (*L. Schilleriana* × *L. Skinneri*).

## MASDEVALLIA

At the present time Masdevallias do not occupy a prominent position among cultivated Orchids, and this fact is probably due to the great increase of hybrids in such popular genera as Lælia, Cattleya, Cypripedium, and Odontoglossum. A few of the Masdevallias are showy when freely flowered and represented by large specimens, but in the majority of species the flowers are far more quaint and interesting than beautiful. Twenty or twenty-five years ago Masdevallias were much more frequently met with in collections than now; indeed, at the present time numbers of Orchid collections do not contain a single representative of the genus.

Masdevallias are largely found in Columbia at a considerable elevation, and therefore most of them are "cool" Orchids, and may be grown with the Odontoglossums for the greater part of the year, and afforded five degrees higher temperature during the Winter. The plants suffer from black spotting in the leaves if they are kept too cool and moist during the dull months. All the species are of tufted growth, evergreen, and have no pseudo-bulbs. They succeed in the ordinary mixture of peat and sphagnum, but do not need a large amount of potting material. August or early September is a good time to pot most of the species, but if the work cannot be done then, so as to give the plants a chance of becoming re-established before Winter sets in, it should be deferred until February. The section of which *M. Chimæra* may be

LYCASTE  SKINNERI  HELLEMENSE.

regarded as the type have more or less pendulous flowers, and are best accommodated in baskets and grown at the coolest end of the intermediate house.

Although Masdevallias are now relegated to a secondary position, there are about a dozen species and hybrids that are deserving of attention where space permits or personal taste demands, in fact there is a fine opportunity for amateurs to gain fame in the Orchid World by cultivating Masdevallias in first-rate style and exhibiting the results of their skill before the public.

Masdevallias have their three sepals joined together at the base, except in the *M. Chimæra* group, and the tips of the sepals are usually extended into long slender "tails"; this gives the flowers a curious appearance, and an outline that is roughly tri-angular. In most cases the flowers are borne singly on slender stems, and they vary in size from the minute *M. muscosa* up to the large *M. macrura* and *M. Chimæra*.

### Best Species and Hybrids

M. AMABILIS, a small grower, with orange and carmine flowers. M. ARMINII, rose, shaded with purple, finely grown in the Burford Lodge collection at Dorking. M. BELLA, pendulous, dull yellow, heavily spotted with purple-brown, and with purple-brown tails; must be grown with *M. Chimæra*. M. CAUDATA, buff-yellow and rose. M. CHELSONI, orange and mauve, a fine hybrid between *M. Veitchiana* and *M. amabilis*. M. CHIMÆRA, pendulous, tawny yellow with violet-purple spots and tails; this species has numerous varieties, notably M. C. BACKHOUSEANA, M. C. GORGONA, M. C. SEVERA, and M. C. WALLISII. M. COCCINEA is one of the very best species from a horticultural point of view; the flowers are brilliant scarlet, shaded with rose on the tube and the upper sepal; it, too, has numerous varieties, which show some difference of colour and marking, but all are very attractive and bright; the best are M. c. ACANTHIFOLIA, M. c. ATROPURPUREA, M. c. ATROSANGUINEA, M. c. BULL'S BLOOD, M. c. DENNISONIANA, M. c. GRANDIFLORA, M. c. HARRYANA, one of the finest; M. c. LINDENII; M. c. ROSEA; and M. c. VIOLACEA.    M. DAVISII, bright yellow and orange.    M. IGNEA, red with crimson veins, allied to *M. coccinea*, and well represented by the varieties M. I. AURANTIACA, M. I. BODDAERTIANA, and M. I. MILITARIS.    M. MACRURA, the giant of the family, has erect stems, and leaves over a foot high, and large, bright, tawny yellow flowers that are dotted freely with blackish purple.    M. REICHENBACHIANA, red tube, yellow upper sepal, with whitish lower sepals and green tails; an attractive and free-flowering species.    M. TOVARENSIS, a little gem, with pure white flowers borne several together on six-inch stems; this does well in the cool house, and when the flowers have faded they should be removed, but the spike or stem must not be cut, as such spikes frequently flower a second time.    M. VEITCHIANA, large, vermilion, with tiny purple hairs that give a pretty flush to the flowers; one of the best for general cultivation.

### OTHER SPECIES AND HYBRIDS

The following are all interesting and have a peculiar beauty of their own :—M. CALURA, M. CARDERI, M. CAUDATA-ESTRADÆ, M. COURTAULDIANA, M. CUCULLATA, M. DEMISSA, M. EPHIPPIUM, M. ESTRADÆ, M. FLORIBUNDA, M. IONOCHARIS, M. LUDIBUNDA, M. MOOREANA, M. MEASURESIANA, M. MUSCOSA, M. ROLFEANA, M. ROSEA, M. SCHLIMII, M. SCHRŒDERIANA, M. TRIANGULARIS, M. TRIARISTELLA, M. TROGLODYTES, M. WAGENERIANA, and M. XANTHINA.

MASDEVALLIAS.

## MAXILLARIA

Another large genus, containing remarkably few plants of horticultural merit, although to lovers of the curious a fairly large number of species will appeal. With the exception of one, perhaps two, the members of this family may well be left to those who value a large number of distinct species rather than a collection of fewer plants of high decorative value. These two species represent two distinct groups of the family. MAXILLARIA SANDERIANA has fleshy flowers about six inches across, borne singly on decumbent stems; the plant grows about a foot high, or rather more, and has stout leaves. It is best grown in a basket, in peat and sphagnum, placed in the intermediate house. The other species, and one for which the writer has a weakness, is M. HOUTTEANA, and this has ascending rhizomes, and so is in some sense a climber. All the members of its section should be grown against a piece of tree-fern stem, or up a teak raft, with a little peat and sphagnum about their roots. In M. SANDERIANA the colour is white, with deep and rich blood-red markings at the base of each segment. In M. HOUTTEANA the flowers are smaller and more spreading than in the latter, and the colour is green, with heavy markings of deep crimson-brown.

Of less value, and belonging to the *M. Sanderiana* group, are M. FUCATA, M. GRANDIFLORA, M. SCURRILIS, M. LUTEO-ALBA, M. PICTA (a very free-flowering, sweetly fragrant species, with rather small, yellowish, purple-spotted flowers), M. STRIATA, and M. VENUSTA. Species of note belonging to the *M. Houtteana* group are M. TENUIFOLIA, M. MELEAGRIS, M. SANGUINEA, and M. VARIABILIS.

## MILTONIA

Although the Miltonias are a comparatively small family, natives of Brazil and Colombia, they include a large proportion of species that rank high among free-flowering plants. They are not difficult to cultivate, though it is not always easy to find a place that just suits the pretty *M. Roezlii*. All the kinds are readily increased by division if the work is done at potting time. An intermediate temperature suits them at all times, and it is therefore advisable to cultivate most of them with the Cattleyas during the Winter, and place them at the warmest end of the Odontoglossum house during the Summer. Good fibrous peat serves as a rooting medium, but the fine particles should be removed before use. The addition of sphagnum is not essential, but most growers add it to the extent of one-third of the mixture. There are several small differences of cultural treatment to be observed, as hardly any two species are a success under precisely the same conditions, but the general principles of plenty of water during free growth, and much less moisture when the plants are more or less dormant, must be kept in mind, remembering that Miltonias are never wholly leafless, and therefore must not be severely rested.

If there is one Orchid more than another that those insidious little pests, the Thrips, seem to love, it surely is *Miltonia vexillaria*, and every pains must be taken to keep the plants clean, or failure will inevitably follow. Frequent sponging with soapy water will keep the leaves clean, but even then the pests may sometimes get down into the heart of the new growth, and breed there with alarming speed and freedom, and in a few days do a great deal of harm, eating away the leaf tissue and crippling the tender new leaves. This at once suggests the advisability of regularly dipping

A FINE VARIETY OF LYCASTE SKINNERII.

the plants in X.L.-All or other approved insecticide. It does not take long to dip a few dozen plants, but, of course, the insecticide must on no account be allowed to drain down to the roots of the plant, or much more harm than good will result from the dipping. When the plants have been held in the insecticide for a few seconds, take them out and lay them on their side while the others are being dealt with; when all have been dipped, those first treated will probably be dry enough to be stood upright in their usual positions.

Although Miltonias love plenty of light, they do not like brilliant sunshine, hence thin shading is necessary during the bright Summer days. The leaves of several species are pale, glaucous, or yellowish green, and this light colouring must not be taken as indicating lack of vitality, as it would in the case of plants which have leaves that are naturally of a deep green hue.

### BEST SPECIES AND HYBRIDS

M. CANDIDA has large red-brown, yellow-barred flowers, with a white, purple blotched lip. It grows very well with the Odontoglossums, but should be given a higher temperature after it has flowered (in the Autumn), until the following Spring.

M. CUNEATA flowers in the Spring, and it has red-brown flowers, but the white lip is rosy at the base.

M. ROEZLII is a charming Orchid, and one that needs stove treatment all the year round, and must always be kept moist at the roots. It has white flowers, with a yellow base to the lip and a purple blotch at the base of each petal. As M. ROEZLII is continually making new growths, it flowers both in Spring and Autumn, and where a number of plants are grown, flowers are rarely absent the year through. This is a smaller growing species than most of the others, and seldom exceeds a foot in height.    It needs a shaded position and plenty of atmospheric moisture. Thrips and red spider are its natural enemies.    M. R. ALBA is pure white, save for the yellow base of the lip.

M. REGNELLII is white, with rosy shading towards the base of the sepals and petals, while the lip is rose, marked with purple and bordered with white.    It flowers in the Autumn, and is best treated like *M. candida*.

M. SPECTABILIS is a low grower, and its spikes seldom carry more than one flower.    In the type the sepals and petals are cream-coloured, and the broad lip is rosy-purple, margined with pale rose or white.    M. S. MORELIANA is one of the finest forms of this variable species, and it has a very deep purple lip; M. S. ATRO-RUBENS is even more richly coloured than M. S. MORELIANA, while M. S. VIRGINALIS is white, with a rosy mark at the base of the lip.

M. VEXILLARIA is the most popular member of the family, and it is a fine decorative plant for flowering in the Spring and early Summer.    Two spikes generally proceed from the same pseudo-bulb, and these carry from three to eight or nine large, flat flowers, of a soft rose or rosy lilac shade.    In this, as in many other species, the lip is by far the most prominent organ, and a breadth of three inches is quite common.    After they have flowered the plants should be placed at the warmest end of the Odontoglossum house, or similar position, but when the cool days of Autumn, arrive they must be returned to an intermediate house. Potting may be done about August, when new growth commences, but water must be given sparingly until the new year has brought an increase of light, and flower spikes begin to form.    Some growers defer potting until early in the new year, and this prac-tice should be followed where the plants are grown in or near large towns, and where the light is very weak throughout the

MILTONIA ST. ANDRE.

dull months of the year. M. VEXILLARIA is variable; M. v. ALBA or *M. v. virginalis* has white flowers; M. v. CHELSIENSIS is deeply coloured, and so is M. v. CRIMSON KING; M. v. COBBIANA is pink, with a white lip; M. v. DAISY HAYWOOD is particularly fine, lightly rose tinted on the sepals and petals, and with a yellow base to the big white lip; M. v. LEOPOLDII is deep rose, with a dark maroon blotch at the base of the lip; and M. v. MEMORIA G. D. OWEN is bright rose with a dark rich crimson-purple base to each segment; it is a fine and strikingly distinct variety. There are numerous other varieties, but these are among the finest.

M. BLEUANA is the finest hybrid (*M. vexillaria* x *M. Roezlii*); the sepals and petals are white, shaded with rose at the base, and the broad white lip has a handsome red-brown blotch at the base, extending in front of the yellow disk. M. B. AUREA has a conspicuously large yellow disk, and M. B. NOBILIOR is larger than the original hybrid, and is pure white except for the large, rayed red-brown blotch and the deep yellow disk on the lip. M. ST ANDRE (*M. Roezlii* x *M. Bleuana var.*), is a very pretty hybrid recently raised.

## OTHER SPECIES AND HYBRIDS

M. BLUNTII is supposed to be a natural hybrid between *M. spectabilis* and *M. Clowesii*; it produces its yellow and brown flowers in the late Summer. M. CLOWESII resembles *C. candida*, but flowers in the Autumn. M. FLAVESCENS has yellowish flowers. M. PHALÆNOPSIS has white, purple-streaked flowers. M. SCHRŒDERIANA has brown and yellow sepals and petals, and a white and purple lip; it is a rare Costa Rican species. M. WARSCEWICZII is red-brown, with a rose and white lip on which the red-brown basal blotch is very bright and distinct; M. W. WELTONI is a stronger grower than the type, and has a good deal of yellow in its flowers.

## ODONTIODA

There is no more remarkable development among Orchids than the production of the Odontiodas by crossing Cochlioda (chiefly *C. Nœtzliana*) with species of Odontoglossum. This new hybrid family contains many charming plants, and in nearly every case the flowers have orange or scarlet colouring, showing in a marked degree the influence of *Cochlioda Nœtzliana*. Before long, when the present plants have grown stronger and produce full-sized flowers and spikes, and when some secondary hybrids have been obtained with the size of a fine Odontoglossum, and practically the colour of *C. Nœtzliana*, then the addition of this family will be even more remarkable than at present, and this seems sure to come to pass, and we shall have then what to all intents and purposes are scarlet or orange-scarlet Odontoglossums. The Odontiodas need the same conditions and treatment as Odontoglossums, but should be grown at the warmest end of the cool house.

The hybrids are not numerous at present, and only a few of the leading raisers offer them for sale. Mons. Vuylsteke, of Ghent, was the first to show an Odontioda, and his first effort was O. VUYLSTEKÆ (*C. Nœtzliana* x *O. nobile*). He was soon followed by Messrs Charlesworth & Co. with O. HEATONENSIS (*C. sanguinea* x *O. cirrhosum*), O. BRADSHAWIÆ (*C. Nœtzliana* x *O. crispum*), and O. BOHNHOFFIÆ (*C. vulcanica* x *O. cirrhosum*). Later introductions are O. CHARLESWORTHII (*C. Nœtzliana* x *O. Harryanum*), O. ST FUSCIEN (*C. Nœtzliana* x *O. Adrianæ*), O. THWAITESII (*C. vulcanica* x *O. Harryana*), O. GRAIRIANA (*C. Nœtzliana* x *O. Rossii majus*), O. LUTETIA (*C. Nœtzliana* x

*O. luteo-purpurea*), and a few others, with several remarkably fine varieties of some of the hybrids mentioned, notably O. BRADSHAWIÆ COOKSON'S VARIETY, these latter having been raised from particularly fine forms of the Odontoglossum parent.     Additions to the family continue to arrive, and some splendid hybrids were exhibited at the Temple Show of 1910, as O. KING GEORGE V. and O. ROYAL GEM (*O. Vuylstekeæ* x *Odontoglossum armainvillierense* (*ardentissimum*).

## ODONTOGLOSSUM

An amateur Orchid grower usually commences his modest collection with the Cypripediums that succeed under cool conditions, and having achieved some success with them, and derived a great deal of pleasure and satisfaction from their culture, he looks round for other subjects upon which to exercise his skill.     Already he will have cast longing eyes upon the graceful arching spikes of the wondrously beautiful Odontoglossums grown by his friends, or those exhibited by the leading trade and amateur growers at the meetings of the Royal Horticultural Society and the Manchester Orchid Society, or at the leading provincial shows, and the one species, with its innumerable varieties, that will have attracted his special attention, is *O. crispum*.     This fascinating Orchid has much to answer for. It has lured men to their death, it has tempted fanciers to pay enormous sums of money for a rare and distinctly marked variation from the general type, and it has induced many a lover of flowers to make his or her first attempt at Orchid culture.

Not to admire Odontoglossums seems to be quite outside the bounds of possibility. There is a grace and beauty in the spikes and flowers of these lovely Orchids rarely, if ever, found in any other class of plants.     The blooms are not large enough to be heavy or lumpy, and yet they are so formed in regard to substance and texture that they last ten days or more in water after being cut.    In the bouquets of the bride and her maids, in the offering of love, or in the basket of flowers wherewith we do honour to a gracious and benevolent lady, or one gifted in the art of music, Odontoglossums frequently take a beautiful part.    One flower is a suitable buttonhole bouquet for a gentleman, while a portion of a spike forms a charming spray for a lady to wear at any time.

But while *O. crispum* is the Queen of cool Orchids, it must not be forgotten that the genus includes many other lovely species, as easily cultivated, and that many of these species have numerous varieties, and besides all these there is a great host of hybrids, almost all of which are exquisitely and brilliantly beautiful.    This all goes to show that Odontoglossums are sufficient in themselves to provide abundant material for all the time an enthusiastic amateur can give to their culture and study.    Odontoglossums may well (as in fact they do) form the subject of a most pleasur able, fascinating, and interesting hobby.

Within certain limits these Orchids show a great diversity of form and colour, as well as of size and habit of growth.    The largest flowers are those of *O. grande.*    In the finer forms of *O. crispum,* and in *O. nebulosum, O. Rossii, O. Cervantesii, O. citrosmum,* and *O. coronarium,* the flowers have a more or less rounded outline, and approximate most nearly to the florist's ideal of a flower.    On the other hand, such species as *O. cirrhosum, O. blandum, O. odoratum, O. naevium,* and *O. hastilabium,* produce narrow-petalled and spidery flowers.    The spikes differ considerably in stature and style; *O. Rossii* flowers quite close to the base of the pseudo-bulb, while *O. Edwardii* will produce spikes 5 ft. or more in height.    *O. crispum* is a good example of an arching spike.    *O. nobile* (*O. Pescatorei*) and *O. ardentissimum* usually have long and branching spikes; *O. bictoniense* and *O.*

ODONTIODA BRADSHAWIÆ COOKSONII.

*Uro-Skinneri* each send up an erect inflorescence, and the sweetly-scented *O. citrosmum* differs from the rest in having pendulous spikes, and also in producing these simultaneously with the appearance of the new pseudo-bulb.

Where do these flowers hail from? They are found on the Pacific side of the American Continent, keeping to the vast mountain ranges of the Andees, and ranging from about lat. 20° North to lat. 15° South, or, roughly, from Colima, at the Southern end of the Sierra Madre, in Mexico, down to Cuzco, in Peru. But the region in which the Odontoglossums seem most to congregate is along the Eastern Cordillera of the Andes, from Bogota Northward and North-eastward. Here, in Colombia and Venezuela, but chiefly in the former, are the homes of such splendid species as *O. crispum, O. nobile (Pescatorei), O. luteo-purpureum,* and *O. triumphans. O. citrosmum* comes from towards the Northern limit of the genus; *O. grande* is found in Guatemala; *O. Hallii* from below Quito, almost under the Equator; and *O. cirrhosum, O. Kegeljani (polyxanthum),* and *O. Edwardii* each extend the range farther Southward.

The surprising part of the matter is that, although these Odontoglossums are found (perhaps I should use the word "were" instead of "are," because many of the species cannot be found where they were originally discovered, and some have not been found at all for several years past, owing to the devastation caused by collectors, and in a lesser degree by the progress of civilisation, in Tropical America), they can be grown successfully under quite cool conditions, with very few exceptions. The reason this is so is to be found in the fact that Odontoglossums grow at a considerable elevation, the majority being found from 5000 ft. to 9000 ft. above sea level. This means that the temperature ranges from 40° Fahr. at night up to 90° Fahr. in the middle of the day, according to the season of the year.  Throughout the whole of the Odontoglossum region the atmosphere is heavily charged with moisture almost all the year round, though the Mexican species experience a more distinctly drying or resting season than those found in the Colombian region, the latter, even in the " dry season," rarely passing through twenty-four hours without rain.

Another point of interest is that Odontoglossums grow for the most part in forests composed largely of trees belonging to the Cinchona, Walnut, and Oak families.  These forests are dense and evergreen, consequently the sun's rays, though often prac- tically vertical, have to filter through the leaves ere they reach the Orchids.  But collectors tell us that the plants are most numerous where ravines or streams break up the general level and density of the forest, and it is at such points the air circulates the most freely and the light penetrates the most readily to the plants.  There is also a good deal of difference in the size of the pseudo-bulbs of plants that grow in these lighter positions, as compared with those growing in deeper shade; under the influence of greater shade the pseudo-bulbs are considerably longer than where there is more light, but this does not necessarily mean the spikes are stronger or the flowers larger.

Sorry-looking things are Odontoglossums when they arrive in temperate countries after a long journey through the tropics. Torn ruthlessly from their homes, roots broken and leaves cut away, they suffer many indignities, and frequently they are exposed to the sun for some time, so that excess of moisture is extracted from them.  This treatment is necessary, so that when the plants are finally packed in dry material for their long journey, there is little risk of damage from damp and its attendant evils of fermenta- tion and over-heating.  When packed very green, there is a great danger of Orchids commencing to grow while on the journey, and

ODONTOGLOSSUM CRISPUM

such growth, made in the dark, can seldom be saved, or, if saved, is of little use.

Assuming the beginner decides to start right away with imported Odontoglossums, then a few dozen should be purchased at the Orchid Sale Rooms, or through the medium of one of the nurserymen who make a speciality of Orchids and Orchid culture. When the plants arrive there will be intense disappointment unless the purchaser is already acquainted with the appearance of imported Odontoglossums. However, the first thing to do after unpacking is to spread out the plants on the bench in the potting shed or greenhouse, preferably the former, and examine each one carefully. The removal of all decaying matter is work of the first importance, and ought to be followed by a thorough cleansing of pseudo-bulbs and stems, so that any insects hiding snugly may be ousted, and the subsequent new growth have the full benefit of a clean start in life. These little attentions are all in the day's work of an Orchid specialist, but they are apt to be omitted by the novice, who, perchance, may have to pay rather heavily for the omission, either in trouble with pests or the rotting of new growths, or both.

The next business is to give the plants a chance to grow, and this is best done by laying them out on a bed of sphagnum moss in the house where they are to be cultivated. If the moss is kept moist by means of tepid water, the conditions provided will be suitable; only during very fine and warm weather should the plants be lightly sprayed with tepid water. Much heat given at this period in the hope that the dormant plants will start into growth more quickly, and profit thereby, will defeat the end in view. In a few weeks indications of renewed vitality will be clearly seen at the base of many of the pseudo-bulbs, and before long new growths will appear. The temptation to hurry off to the potting shed for pots and potting material as soon as these growths are seen is a great and pardonable one, but it must not on any account be yielded to. Let us think a moment. Here are rootless and leafless plants, with their fleshy bodies still further weakened by a long journey through hot regions, and by being packed in dry material. They are invalids just taking a turn for the better, but by no means fit for strong diet. "Make haste slowly" is an excellent motto to bear in mind at this stage.

The proper time to pot newly imported Odontoglossums is when the new growths have made some progress and new roots are being formed at the base. It is useless to expect all the plants will be ready for potting at the same time; some will soon begin to grow and root, while others wait a long time before showing any signs of life. The plants must be potted as they become ready for that process. Large specimens are very rarely imported nowadays, consequently large pots will not be required. The size of pot to use is one that will just comfortably accommodate the plant to be dealt with. Three inch (60's), or four and a half inch (48's), will usually be large enough for the Odontoglossums obtained to start with.

Use clean pots, and if the pots are new ones, they must be soaked in a tank of water for at least an hour or two (and then drained and dried) before being used. When established, and especially when growing freely, Odontoglossums need an abundance of moisture, and as the material in which they are potted has, with very few exceptions, to be kept moist all the year round, it will be readily understood that there must be ample drainage beneath the compost to permit the water applied above to pass quickly away. If the water does not pass away readily, the compost will become sour, the root tips be killed, and the plant die or become seriously weakened. The old practice was to place

A YOUNG ODONTOGLOSSUM PLANT (WITH NEW GROWTH)

one potsherd concavely over the drainage hole, and cover this to one-third or one-half the pot's depth with smaller potsherds or crocks, but the modern method is to place a large crock in the bottom of the pot and cover it to the depth of an inch or so with small pieces of the rhizomes of the common Bracken fern.   These rhizomes are found in the turves of peat supplied by the nurserymen, or they may be purchased separately, provided one has no access to a Common or Heath or Woodland where this most common of British ferns is abundant.   The rhizomes must be sterilized before use, otherwise they may grow and cause trouble.

Sterilization is easily managed by putting the rhizomes in a very hot oven long enough to kill them, or by placing a quantity in a copper full of boiling water for a few minutes, and then spreading them out to dry.

A great deal might be written about the material or materials in which the Odontoglossums are to root.   The fibrous portion of the peat cut from Moor or Common, and consisting chiefly of the fine Heather and Bracken roots, was long regarded as the only suitable material for Odontoglossums, and there are still many successful growers who use nothing else, saving always the addition of Sphagnum moss.   But Polypodium, Osmunda, and other fern fibres have been used with excellent results in place of peat during recent years, while the *terre bruyère* of the Belgians has had a great vogue on the Continent.   Half-decayed leaves (not leaf mould as we generally understand it), is now very largely used, and in the hands of numerous skilful cultivators it has proved an eminently successful potting material.   It consists of Oak or Beech leaves, collected as soon as they have fallen in the Autumn, and stored free from other leaves, soil, or sweepings.   If heavy rains are kept from them, they will be in good condition for use the following Autumn, and the only preparation necessary will consist of lightly rubbing them between the hands and sifting out the finer portions. I have seen Odontoglossums growing luxuriantly in this sort of leaf mould in Belgium, and potted just in the same manner we should follow when potting bedding Pelargoniums.

As the leaves hold water more than peat, and as they decay quicker, there is the ever-present danger of over-watering, or the retention of an excess of moisture about the roots of the plants. Leaves used as a rooting medium encourage free root action, big pseudo-bulbs, and large leaves and spikes.     But there are not wanting those who assert that the flowers so produced lack substance and are not long-lived, while the plants suffer far more than peat-grown ones if taken into the dwelling-house for a time, or if exhibited at a flower show.    The slow evaporation and poor light that obtain in and near large towns during the Winter do not suit the comparatively sappy growth made by Odontoglossums cultivated in leaves, but out in the country, where the better light helps to consolidate these growths, the results are often very fine. Beginners should stick to peat and sphagnum for the potting mixture until they are no longer beginners, but have sufficient experience to handle new materials discreetly.    If they are venturesome they may add a quite small proportion (one-fifth of the whole bulk) of leaves to the peat and sphagnum.

To show an amateur how to pot an imported Odontoglossum would be an easy task, but to describe the operation in words is quite another matter.  After mixing the broken peat with an equal amount of clean, roughly-chopped sphagnum, allow the mixture to remain in the house all one night, so that it is at the same temperature as the atmosphere by the time potting is begun. Commence bv placing a good layer of the potting compost over the drainage material, building it up in the centre of the pot, so that the base of the plant will be raised by it a little above the

ODONTOGLOSSUM ROSSII RUBESCENS.

level of the rim.   Then, keeping the plant in the centre, proceed to fill in the compost around it, beginning at one side and working round, making the compost firm with the fingers, or by means of a short stick, as the work proceeds.   The stick must not be used as a rammer, but simply to press the compost firmly and sideways. An experienced grower would be able to pot an Odontoglossum with this compost pretty much as others would pot a Pelargonium, without making the material too hard and compact, but the usual practice is to proceed on the lines suggested.   When potted, the plant should stand firmly in the centre of the pot, and, as suggested, a little raised above the rim level.   But at the margin the compost should be a little below the rim of the pot, so that when water is given it passes through the compost and does not run off it.   A pair of scissors or small shears will enable the operator to trim away loose pieces of sphagnum or peat fibre, and give a finished appearance to the work.   A few heads of fresh, green sphagnum may be dibbled in, but this is a matter of appearance rather than of necessity.   Watering with soft tepid water through a very fine rose will complete the business.

When established plants are in need of more root room, their needs should be supplied.   The work of re-potting is but a modification of the potting process already described.   The retention or rejection of the old pseudo-bulbs is a subject for consideration, because after a few years these may become so numerous as to occupy a large amount of room in the pot.   All pseudo-bulbs still carrying leaves should be retained, but behind these not more than one, or at most two, need be allowed to remain.   Sever the rhizome or underground stem with a sharp knife, between the portions to be retained and rejected.   A clean pot and clean, fresh drainage must be provided for the plant that is to be re-potted, and before it is put in the new material, all the old potting compost should be carefully removed from its roots.   Cut away decayed roots, be careful not to damage good roots, and keep a sharp look-out for insect pests that may lurk in the sheltering base of old leaf sheaths.

There are two " best times " for re-potting Odontoglossums ; one is February and the other September.   In a general sense the latter is the best time, because the climate at that season of the year is usually genial, *i.e.* not cold or very hot, but pleasantly mild, with an absence of brilliant, scorching sunshine, and the presence of a moist atmosphere, caused by gentle showers and dewy nights.   These eminently suitable conditions encourage the plants to root freely into the new compost, and so they re-establish themselves quickly, and are well able to withstand the trials of the succeeding Winter.   But the trials of Winter are nothing (except in and near large towns) compared to the severe strain our bright dry Summers impose upon Odontoglossums.   Plants not needing to be re-potted in September may be in want of attention in the early Spring ; if so, they should be re-potted in February, so that they may become re-established before the drying days of Summer arrive.   Where the plants do not require more root room, and the potting compost is still in good condition, a renovation of the surface may be desirable.   This is managed by removing a little of the surface material, and putting new peat and sphagnum (the latter chiefly), in its place.   This does not take long, and it adds to the tidy and smart appearance of the collection, whether it be a large or a small one.

Watering Odontoglossums is not the serious affair some people would have us think.   Why so many good folk try their level best to surround the whole subject of Orchid culture with an air of impenetrable mystery, I fail to understand, especially when it is no uncommon thing to find Orchids growing and flowering

splendidly in gardens where there are but few Orchids of any kind, and where there is no pretence made of understanding even these few.  A careful consideration of the annual round of a plant's life is essential if we are to be successful in its cultivation.  Cattleyas cannot succeed if treated like Phalaenopsis; some of the Mexican Odontoglossums must be treated differently to the Colombian species; but then the same idea holds good in other families of plants.  For instance, it is painfully easy to come a cropper with the beautiful Hippeastrums, especially if their natural conditions of life are deliberately ignored, and they are given the same conditions as either *Amaryllis Belladonna*, *Crinum giganteum*, *Hæmanthus sanguinea*, or *Agave americana*, all of which belong to the same Natural Order, and are therefore related to the Hippeastrums.  The mistakes mostly made are not those of temperature, but those of watering.

When an imported Odontoglossum is potted, or an established plant is re-potted, neither will need much water at the roots until root action is vigorous.  A moist atmosphere and comparatively little ventilation for a fortnight after the operation will assist the plants, and obviate the need of much water to keep the potting compost moist.  When an Odontoglossum has flowered, and the spike has been removed, it should have a reduced water supply for a few weeks, but the supply must not be so reduced as to cause the pseudo-bulbs to shrivel or the leaves to fall.  This treatment will have the effect of giving the plant a short rest, but it must not be prolonged.  At the first sign of new growth, or with a view of inducing new growth to start, moister rooting conditions must soon be resorted to; but it is while growth and root action are both free that the largest supply of water will be needed.  Every plant must be dealt with according to its immediate condition and needs.  It is impossible to succeed with Odontoglossums if the batch or house of plants is treated as a mass much in the same general way that we treat a bed of Cabbages, instead of being considered and cared for as so many individuals.

Temperature and ventilation are matters that must be considered together.     It is a fatal mistake to believe ventilation is chiefly for the reduction of temperature.     It is not.     The chief end of ventilation is to supply the plants with plenty of fresh air. Fixed temperatures are also a great mistake.     In the Odontoglossum house the Winter temperature should range from 45° to 55° at night, and from 50° to 60° by day, the lowest night reading being reached on very cold, windy or frosty nights, and the highest day reading being reached on mild and bright days. During the Summer the night figures should be 50° to 55°, and the day figures 55° to 65°.     The latter figure will be often reached, and probably often exceeded, in the hottest part of the Summer.     With high temperature and plenty of ventilation there must be a free distribution of water among the pots and over floors and wall spaces.     This process of " damping down " may have to be performed half a dozen times on hot, dry days, while a thorough hosing of the paths outside the house will at such times temper the dryness of the air.     Ventilation by means of the ventilators set in the highest part of the house (top ventilators), is not an unmixed blessing, because the free circulation creates a very dry atmosphere, therefore this sort of ventilation must be given with great discretion.     Bottom ventilation is safer in two ways.     In the Winter the air admitted through the bottom ventilators is warmed by its contact with the hot-water pipes, which are usually set under the side or front stages.     In the Summer time it is possible to have these lower ventilators open on both sides of the house, consequently, if there is plenty of moisture-holding material on the stages and also on the floor spaces

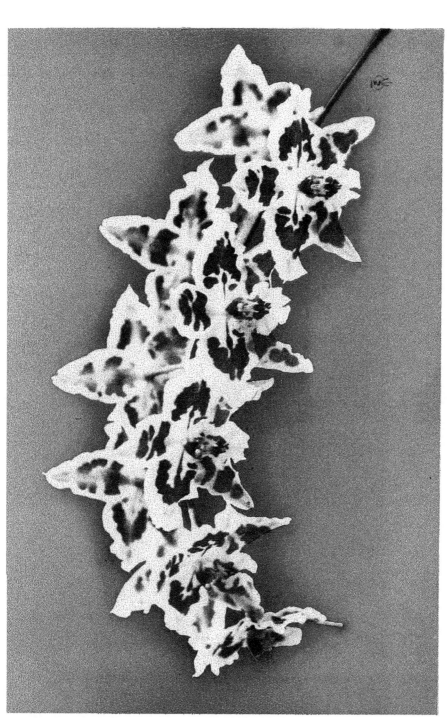

ODONTOGLOSSUM × LAINVILLIERENSE (RIDENTISSIMUM), WESTONBIRT VARIETY.

under the pipes and staging, the air is moistened, and refreshes the plants.

Artificial heating is unnecessary for Odontoglossums during July and August in most parts of the country. It may probably be dispensed with a little earlier, and a little later also, in many districts. Bottom ventilation, fairly heavy shading, and the shading kept six inches or so above the glass, ought, with plenty of moisture about the house, to keep the temperature within reasonable limits during the hottest part of a hot Summer's day. At such a time give little or no top ventilation, but during the cool of the evening open the top ventilators for a while, closing them down a good deal, but not shutting them, the last thing at night. They should be shut down first thing in the morning when the floors and stages are damped and the shading brought into use.

The selection of species and hybrids for the purpose of commencing a collection is an interesting and serious business. The best dozen species for a beginner—indeed the best for anyone, are O. CIRRHOSUM, O. CRISPUM, O. EDWARDII, O. GRANDE, O. HALLII, O. HARRYANUM, O. HASTILABIUM, O. LUTEO-PURPUREUM, O. NOBILE (PESCATOREI), O. KEGELJANI (POLYXANTHUM), O. ROSSII, and O. TRIUMPHANS.

O. CIRRHOSUM has rather narrow segments, and these are elongated into fine tail-like ends. The colour is white, lightly strewn with deep maroon spots and dots. An elegant and pretty species.

O. CRISPUM is so variable as to be beyond description in a line or two, but its general character is so well known to all who are interested in flowers, that a detailed description is not necessary. In general terms, the flowers are white with a few red or chocolate spots on the lip, and a yellow crest at the base of the lip. Sometimes the flowers are more or less tinted or shaded with rose, while in other cases the white ground colour is almost obliterated by large blotches of purple or deep red.     Varieties of the purest and unspotted white, if of fine rounded form, are rare, beautiful, and expensive; but far more valuable are the heavily blotched and deeply coloured varieties, and for extraordinarily fine varieties of this kind, sums ranging from £250 to £1000 have been paid. In a batch of thousands of imported plants scarcely will any two be quite alike, so variable is this wonderful Orchid.     Some will have thin, spidery flowers, and be hardly worth growing, but plenty will be of good useful size, substance, and character, and a few, maybe, will be well above the average.     A beginner may start with plants ranging in price from £5 to £25 per hundred.     These, whether established or imported plants, will provide plenty of mild excitement, and reward his skill with charming flowers.     The "weedy" varieties will be turned out in due course to make way for the finer ones.     O. C. LEONARD PERFECT, O. C. FRANZ MASE-REEL, O. C. COOKSONII, O. C. SOLUM, O. C. DUKE OF YORK, O. C. AUREUM ROSEFIELDIENSE, and O. C. PITTIANUM are a few of the gems.

O. EDWARDII is a most distinct Odontoglossum, and though its flowers are only an inch across, they are produced in considerable numbers on the long, branching spikes.     The colour, deep purple-mauve, with yellow teeth or crest, is very effective, and the species is always a favourite.

O. GRANDE is rightly named, for it is a grand Orchid when at its best, but it needs rather different treatment to that accorded the O. crispum group.     The large flowers are often six inches broad, and the spikes, which are only a little longer than the stiff leaves, carry from three to seven of these splendid blooms.     The ground colour is bright yellow, the basal half of each petal is brown and the sepals are barred with brown, while the lip is lightly marked with red or brown. During the Summer *O. grande* will do quite well with *O. crispum*, but as Autumn draws in this Orchid must be placed in warmer and drier conditions, given all the light possible, and be kept rather dry all the Winter. It will succeed in an intermediate house during the Winter months, provided it is given very little water and allowed to become quite dry before being watered; or it may be placed for a similar period at the coolest end of the house in which Cattleyas are grown.

O. HALLII is a graceful Spring flowering species from the Quito district, where it was discovered by Col. Hall in 1837, but it was not until about 1864 that it came into cultivation. It is a variable species and bears many flowers on its long, arching spikes. Each bloom is from three to four inches across and of a pale yellow colour, sometimes even white, with bright red-brown spots and blotches, the latter often occupying the greater part of the area of the sepals. The lip may be pale yellow, or even white, with red spots; the fringing along the edge of the lip is also a distinctive character. Notwithstanding its grace and beauty O. Hallii is not so largely grown as formerly, probably because it is not so often imported as some other species, and the popularity of O. crispum and the now plentiful artificial hybrids has also militated against it.

O. HARRYANUM, one of the most distinct of Odontoglossums, is named in honour of that celebrated horticulturist, Mr Harry J. Veitch, of Chelsea. It flowered for the first time in cultivation in August 1886. The species has but one failing, *i.e.* the petals come forward and also turn inward a little, with reflexing tips, and thus partly hide their exquisite basal markings and also the beauty of the base of the lip. In spite of this, however, it is a very fine species, and one that is deservedly popular. Not only does it stand high for its own intrinsic merit, but it has proved of immense value to the hybridist, and its distinctive characters are to be seen in its progeny even to the second and third generation. The sepals are red-brown, margined and tipped with golden yellow and with the latter colour breaking up the former into large blotches. In the petals there is a wonderful combination of yellow, brown, white, and purple, while the large three-lobed lip is white, heavily veined with purple at the base, where the golden yellow, fimbriated crest is a conspicuous object. The front lobe sometimes changes from white to pale yellow.

O. HASTILABIUM is an easily grown species, and one that produces tall branching spikes of elegant flowers. It comes from New Granada, where it was discovered by M. Linden in 1843. It first flowered in this country in 1846, at Syon House, Brentford. About three inches in diameter, the blooms are made up of almost equal sepals and petals, these being rather narrow, pale greenish yellow, freely spotted and lightly barred with purple, except at the tips. The base of the lip, and also the sharply contracted central portion, are purple, but the broad apex is white, and this is by far the most prominent part. Messrs Cypher & Sons, of Cheltenham, frequently use this fine old species to great advantage in their splendid groups of plants at the leading Flower Shows.

O. LUTEO-PURPUREUM is one of the most variable of all the Odontoglossums, and in the earlier days of Orchid culture many of its varietal forms were accorded specific rank, and this led to a good deal of confusion. There is a wide difference between one of the ordinary, dark-marked varieties and the charming O. luteo-purpureum Vuylstekeanum with its two shades of yellow instead of dark brown and yellow. And there is also a great difference in the price, for Vuylsteke's variety is rare, so that a specimen of it would cost £21, while a plant of equal

ODONTOGLOSSUM ROLFEÆ.

size, but of a common type, would be worth 5s.  The flowers measure from three to four inches across, and the colouring is usually bright yellow and red-brown, the latter predominating in the sepals and the yellow in the petals.  The lip may be white or pale yellow, and usually has one or more red spots towards the base.  The species is badly named, as the colouring is never yellow and purple, as the title suggests.

O. NOBILE is still popularly known as *O. Pescatorei*, and was thus named after a wealthy Parisian banker who was a great lover of Orchids, but O. NOBILE is the correct title.  It is a delightful species, and one which a few specialists admire even more than the beautiful *O. crispum*.  Somewhat like the latter, it is, however, even more refined than that popular kind.  The ground colour is white, and on this are markings of bright magenta-purple. Sometimes the purple is only seen as a small mark on the lip, or as a pale shading on the sepals or petals, but in the most highly prized and highly priced varieties it may be in large blotches on the basal half of each segment, as in the case of O. N. VEITCHII, in Baron Schroder's collection, and O. N. CHARLESWORTHII.

O. KEGELJANI (or *O. polyxanthum*, to give it its more popular but incorrect name), one of the writer's favourites, has showy, bright yellow flowers, heavily marked with light brown on the sepals and lip, and more lightly marked on the base of the petals. Discovered in Ecuador in 1877, it first flowered in this country with Mr Walter Cobb, whose collection was then at Sydenham, in 1880.  It has not proved very variable, and probably its general conformity to the type has placed it outside the enthusiasm of those collectors who prize a specimen chiefly because it has an extra spot or a deeper shade of colour than the majority of its kind.

O. ROSSII, a dwarf-growing species, is one that is sure to attract the beginner in Orchid culture, as it has a neat habit and can be well grown in pots or pans suspended from the rafters, and will thus not take up much room. It is a Mexican species, discovered by the collector whose name it bears, and it was introduced in 1837. It varies somewhat, but many of the so-called varietal forms described in the older works on Orchids have since proved to be natural hybrids. When in growth only, O. ROSSII is but a few inches high, and its flower spikes rarely rise above eight or nine inches. There is no mistaking O. ROSSII when once it has been seen, for in no other species is there so great a contrast between the sepals and the petals. The former are rather narrow, and so heavily spotted and blotched with brown, that the whitish or rose coloured ground is almost obliterated. The petals are much broader, white or rose, and with a few brown or purple-brown spots quite at the base. The lip varies in shape, but in the best varieties this segment is broadly heart-shaped, while the colour is white or rose. So charming an Orchid as this is worth a little extra attention, and this it needs, for, like some other Mexican species, it succeeds best when suspended near the roof-glass and wintered in a temperature a few degrees higher than is provided for O. crispum. O. ROSSII RUBENS is a very distinct variety.

O. TRIUMPHANS was discovered by M. Linden in New Granada; it has showy, golden yellow flowers, three inches across, marked with light brown. Mr de Barri Crawshay, of Sevenoaks, has some especially fine varieties with broad petalled flowers, notably O. T. LIONEL CRAWSHAY, O. T. RAYMOND CRAWSHAY, and O. T. ROSEFIELD VARIETY.

### OTHER GOOD SPECIES

Odontoglossums of lesser value than the foregoing might be named by dozens, and probably in a few instances they may be preferred to those here considered more important. It is impossible to select a given number of species and find the set approved by

ODONTOGLOSSUM ELEANOR.

everyone. The following may be added as taste suggests and space permits; indeed, the addition of a few is strongly advised, because of the greater interest they lend to a collection.

O. BICTONENSE has the honour of being the first member of its family to reach England alive; it was introduced in 1835, and first flowered at Bicton, in Devonshire, hence its name. It usually flowers in the Autumn, and carries its blooms on erect spikes; the sepals are green and brown, and the broad heart-shaped lip is rose coloured. O. BLANDUM is a graceful little species, a sort of diminutive *O. cirrhosum*. O. CERVANTESII is another dwarf species, and should be grown in the same manner as *O. Rossii*; its rounded flowers are white, with tangential lines of red-brown at their base. O. CORDATUM has spidery flowers, three or four inches across, yellow with brown marking, except for the lip, which is white with brown spots. O. CORONARIUM is not a difficult Orchid to grow, but it is a difficult one to accommodate, and not an easy one to flower; its pseudo-bulbs are set widely apart, and so a raft or long, trough-shaped basket has to be provided for it. O. CORONARIUM has stiffly erect spikes, and the rounded blooms, nearly three inches across, bright brown, marked with yellow, are very attractive; the variety O. C. MINIATUM has a yellow lip, is of better habit, and more amenable to cultivation than the type.

O. HUNNEWELLIANUM will appeal to some, but is chiefly interesting as being one parent of the popular hybrid *O. Adrianæ*. O. INSLEAYI may be likened to *O. grande*, but it is smaller, and the brown markings are usually darker and more numerous. O. KRAMERI is a dwarf Costa Rican species with small flowers, coloured violet and white. O. LÆVE is a variable species, and produces spikes from two to three feet in length, bearing many flowers that are brown and yellow or greenish yellow, and have a white or rosy lip. This is a fragrant Orchid, and is sometimes

met with under the title of *O. Reichenheimii*.    O. LINDLEYANUM
grows very much like *O. crispum*, and has yellow, brown-blotched
sepals and petals, and a white lip with brown, purple, and yellow
marks.    O. LONDESBOROUGHIANUM is a difficult plant to manage;
it has a rambling habit, much like *O. coronarium*, needs the
warmth of a Cattleya House, plenty of sunshine, and occasionally
deigns to give tall spikes of bright yellow flowers that are lightly
marked with red-brown.    O. MACULATUM resembles *O. cordatum*,
is easily grown, but is hardly so good a plant.    O. NÆVIUM has
slender spikes of elegant white, purple-spotted flowers, and is a
very pretty species.    O. NEBULOSUM produces flowers three inches
across, rounded, white, faintly but freely marked at the base of
the segments with brown, the marks being deepest at the base of
the lip.    O. ODORATUM often passes under the name of *O. gloriosum*,
and at one time the pale-flowered varieties were grouped under
the latter name, and the brighter ones under *O. odoratum*; the
segments are all narrow, and the colour is some shade of light
yellow, with small red-brown markings.    It ought to be grown
more than it is, if only for the sake of its sweet Hawthorn-like
fragrance.

O. OERSTEDII should be grown in shallow pans near the
glass, as it loves good light; its flowers are small, pure white,
except for a tiny yellow mark at the base of the lip.    The pretty
O. PULCHELLUM has white flowers that dispense an odour like that
of Hyacinths.    O. RAMOSISSIMUM is an elegant species, bearing
numerous spidery, wavy flowers, white, freely spotted with bright
purple, on a branching spike two feet or more high.    O.
SCHLIEPERIANUM is well described as intermediate between *O.
grande* and *O. Insleayi*, and should be grown with them.    O.
TRIPUDIANS has bright red-brown flowers, lightly marked with
bright yellow.    O. URO-SKINNERI flowers in the Autumn, and

ODONTOGLOSSUM WILCKEANUM

resembles *O. bictonense*, but has its sepals and petals mottled with green and brown, and its lip speckled with white over rose; it is a fine and very desirable species, and one difficult to exclude from the best dozen.

## THE BEST HYBRIDS

Practically all the hybrid Odontoglossums are of easy culture, and there need be no hesitation in purchasing those that have now been raised in large numbers artificially.   The merit of the plants obtained will, of course, be governed by the price paid, for the progeny of one seed pod will vary greatly, and the more finely coloured and the shapeliest flowers always command the highest prices.   The hybrids add a great variety of form and colour to a collection and they are therefore most desirable.   Very few people, however, can afford to purchase the finest and rarest and newest of these evidences of the hybridist's skill, and it is a mistake, from the point of view of popularising Orchid culture, that so many of our leading raisers exhibit only these more expensive forms, and so the budding enthusiast, who would be delighted with the plants a specialist would despise, is disheartened.

For their beauty, interest, decorative value, and ease of culture the following hybrids are the best for an amateur to select from, and as they all show the principal features of their parents it is not necessary to describe them minutely

O. ADRIANÆ (*O. crispum* x *O. Hunnewellianum*), is usually brown and white or brown and buff; O. A. ASHWORTHIANUM, O. A. ARTHUR ASHWORTH, O. A. ERNEST ASHWORTH, O. A. COUNTESS OF MORLEY, O. A. LADY WIGAN, and O. A. LORD ROBERTS are all fine varieties of this hybrid.

O. AMABILE (*O. crispum* x *O. spectabile*), a fine hybrid in which rose, brown, purple, white and yellow are the chief colours; O. A. GOLIATH, O. A. ROYAL SOVEREIGN, O. A. IXION, and O. A. FOWLER'S VARIETY are fine forms.

O. ANDERSONIANUM (*O. crispum* x *O. odoratum*), is a natural hybrid and it is usually pale yellow with brown spots; O. A. CRAWSHAY'S VARIETY, O. A. CRAWSHAYANUM, O. A. ROSE-FIELDIENSE, and O. A. SUPERBUM are among the chief varieties.

O. ARMAINVILLIERENSE (*O. crispum* x *O. nobile* [*Pescatorei*]), is perhaps better known as *O. ardentissimum*. It is a beautiful hybrid ranging from pure white up to brilliant purple and rose. Some of the finer forms are O. A COOKSONÆ, O. A. HERBERT GOODSON, O. A. VENUS, O. A. THEODORA, O. A. COOKSONI, O. A. APOLLO, and O. A. WESTONBIRT VARIETY.

O. BEAUTÉ-CŒLESTE (*O. armainvillierense* × *O. crispum*), is the hybrid frequently shown as *O. eximium*. It is represented in the finer collections by such beautiful varieties as O. B.-C. KING EDWARD, O. B.-C. QUEEN ALEXANDRA, and O. B.-C. CŒRULEUM.

O. DENISONÆ (*O. crispum* x *O. luteopurpureum*), is the hybrid so well known as *O. Wilckeanum*, but this, as well as *O. Leroyanum*, are but varieties of O. DENISONÆ. It has yellow ground flowers freely marked with red-brown. O. D. COOKSONI, O. D. GODE-FROYÆ, O. D. PITTIÆ, O. D. PITT'S VARIETY, and O. D. QUEEN EMPRESS are fine varieties.

O. ELEANOR (*O. cirrhosum* x *O. Uro-Skinneri*), is one of the newer hybrids, and combines two elegant and interesting species. The WESTONBIRT VARIETY is particularly good.

O. ELEGANS (*O. cirrhosum* × *O. Hallii*), is a rare and costly beauty; it has red, yellow, and white colouring.

O. EXCELLENS (*O. nobile* x *O. triumphans*), is very pretty even in its poorest forms, the yellow, often golden, flowers being spotted with deep brown. Fine varieties are O. E. HYEANUM, O. E.

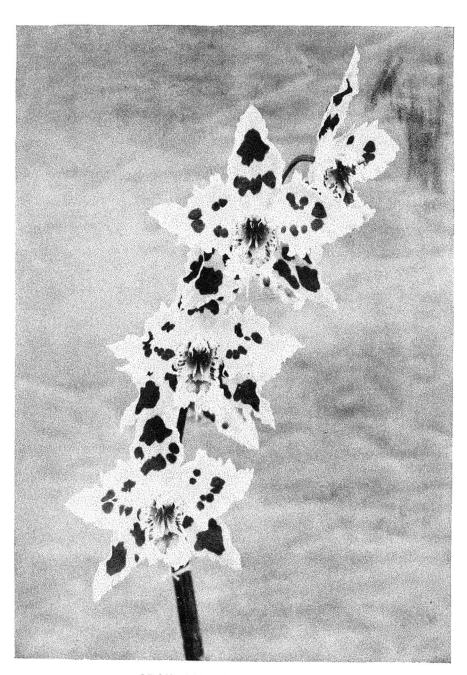

ODONTOGLOSSUM OSSULTONI

McBeaneanum, O. e. Prince of Orange, O. e. Sanderæ, and O. e. Rosslyn variety.

O. harvengtense (*O. crispum* x *O. triumphans*), is identical with *O. loochristiense*, but the former is the earlier title. It has deep yellow, brown marked flowers. O. h. Canary Bird and O. h. Kimberley are fine forms.

O. Japonais (*O. crispum* x *O. Rolfeæ*), is now regarded as the correct title for the beautiful *O. Lambeauianum*. It is very variable, and specially fine varieties are O. J. exquisitum and O. J. The Idol.

O. Ossultoni (*O. nobile* x *O. spectabile*), has very dainty flowers, usually with purple or rose markings on white ground. O. O. Glebelands variety and O. O. W. H. Hatcher are notable forms of the hybrid.

O. percultum (*O. armainvillierense* x *O. Rolfeæ*), like other secondary hybrids, is very variable, but it is always attractive; O. p. Cybele, O. p. Orion, O. p. Cookson's variety, and O. p. J. H. Roberts are notably fine.

O. Phœbe (*O. cirrhosum* x *O. crispum*), is a very elegant hybrid, with red-brown marks on a white ground; O. p. magnificum, and O. p. The Dell variety are its best forms.

O. Rolfeæ (*O. Harryanum* x *O. nobile*), is a very handsome hybrid, and often richly marked with brown, rose, purple, and yellow; some of the best varieties are O. R. Walton Grange variety, O. R. meleagris, and O. R. optimum.

O. spectabile (*O. crispum* x *O. Harryanum*), is the proper title for *O. crispo-Harryanum* and *O. Harryano-crispum*. It is a striking hybrid, in which the influence of *O. Harryanum* is very marked; the variety O. s. King Edward is particularly fine.

O. Thompsonianum (*O. crispum* x *O. Edwardii*), is deep

purple, with narrow white marks. It has a long spike, and shows the influence of *O. Edwardii* in a marked degree.

O. VUYLSTEKEÆ (*O. spectabile* x *O. Vuylstekei*), is a fine hybrid but the parentage given is sometimes doubted; it is rare at present.

O. VUYLSTEKEI (*O. Denisonæ* x *O. triumphans*), has yellow and white flowers, and is very attractive.

O. WALTONENSE (*O. crispum* x *O. Kegeljani*), has clear yellow flowers, with a red-brown mark on the white tipped lip.

### OTHER HYBRIDS

In such a work as this it is impossible to describe all the Hybrid Odontoglossums, or even to enumerate them; but for the purpose of indicating how far the raisers have progressed, a few more are referred to here. Some of these are by no means inferior to many of these previously named, but they are at present rare, and costly in most cases, and therefore only for the amateur with a long purse:—

O. ALICEÆ (*O. Edwardi* x *O. spectabile*), O. AMOENUM (*O. nobile* x *O. sceptrum*), the correct name for *O. concinnum*; O. BELLATULUM (*O. crispum* x *O. tripudians*), O. BRADSHAWIÆ (*O. Andersonianum* x *O. Harryanum*), O. BRANDTIÆ (*O. luteopurpureum* x *O. nobile*), O. CHARLESWORTHII (*O. Harryanum* x *O. triumphans*), probably the same as *O. Queen Alexandra* and *O. Harryano-triumphans*; O. CLYTIE (*O. Edwardii* x *O. nobile*), O. COOKSONÆ (*O. armainvillierense* x *O. percultum*), O. COOKSONI (*O. crispum* x *O. Hallii*), O. CRAWSHAYANUM (*O. Hallii* x *O. Harryanum*), O. ELAINE (*O. cirrhosum* x *O. Harryanum*), O. EURYDICE (*O. cirrhosum* x *O. hastilabium*), O. FASCINATOR (*O. Adrianæ* x *O. crispum*), O. FORMOSUM (*O. nobile* x *O. Rolfeæ*), O. FOWLERIANUM (*O. cirrhosum* x *O. Rossii*), O. GANDAVENSIS (*O. armainvillierense* x

ODONTOGLOSSUM AMABLE.

*O. Vuylstekeæ*), O. GLADYS (*O. cirrhosum* × *O. spectabile*), O. GOODSONI (*O. Uro-Skinneri* × *O. nobile Charlesworthii*), O. GROGANIÆ (*O. Edwardii* x *O. Uro-Skinneri*), O. HALLI-XANTHUM (*O. Hallii* × *O. Kegeljani*), O. HIBERNICUM (*O. Hallii* x *O. hastilabium*), O. HYEANUM (*O. Harryanum* x *O. luteopur-pureum*), a fine hybrid, exhibited as *O. Souv. de Victor Hye de Crom* ; O. ILLUSTRE (*O. Vuylstekei* × *O. armainvillierense var. ardentissimum*), O. LAIRESSEI (*O. Cervantesii* × *O. Edwrdii*), O. LAWRENCEANUM (*O. Rolfeæ* × *O. triumphans*), O. MIRIFICUM (*O. crispum* x *O. sceptrum*), O. MIRUM (*O. crispum* × *O. Denisonæ*), O. OTHELLO (*O. Adrianæ* x *O. Harryanum*), O. SMITHII (*O. Rossii* x *O. spectabile*), O. SYLVIA (*O. cirrhosum* × *O. Rolfeæ*), O. TERPSICHORE (*O. Kegeljani* × *O. nobile*), O. VENUSTULUM (*O. armainvillierense* x *O. spectabile*), O. WATTIANUM (*O. Harryanum* x *O. Lindleyanum*), O. WARNHAMENSE (*O. Hallii* × *O. nobile*), and O. WIGANIANUM (*O. harvengtense* x *O. Rolfeæ*).

## ONCIDIUM

It is unfortunate that some of the most beautiful of the Oncidiums do not continue to thrive under cultivation over a period of several years, but the reason for this is probably to be found in the fact that the species flower with great freedom, and their long, branching spikes impose a great strain upon the plants. The grace and beauty of many species is not surpassed by those of any other Orchids, and it is not therefore surprising that the grower is tempted to enjoy them to the full.   But this means an enormous tax upon the vitality of the plants, and if the spikes are allowed to remain until the flowers fade, the new growths suffer, there is an annual decline in vigour, and newly imported plants have to be obtained to make good the losses.    If as much care was taken to husband the energy of Oncidiums as is done in the case of Odontoglossums, the life of the plants would be greatly prolonged.

Yellow and brown are the colours chiefly found in Oncidiums, and though the flowers are seldom really large, they are freely produced, often in tall, branching spikes, and consequently for grouping, for exhibiting, and for use in the choicest floral designs they are in great demand.    Oncidiums come from Central America, and range from Mexico to Southern Brazil.    Although most of the species resemble Odontoglossums in general habit, there are a few marked differences.    For instance, *O. Cavendishianum* and *O. Lanceanum* have no pseudo-bulbs; *O. macranthum* and its near relatives *O. monachichum*, *O. serratum*, etc., have long, flexuose and branching spikes of fairly large flowers, while *O. Cebolletta* and *O. Jonesianum* have terete, fleshy leaves.

As a general rule Oncidiums need the same cultural conditions as Odontoglossums, but there are exceptions.    *O. ampliatum*, *O. Kramerianum*, *O. Papilio*, and *O. splendidum* require the heat and moisture of the stove, with slightly cooler and drier conditions when at rest.    *O. bracteatum*, *O. flexuosum*, *O. pubes*, *O. sphace-latum*, and *O. sarcodes* do best in an intermediate house, and the writer has seen several of these growing finely in a Muscat Vinery all through the Summer and early Autumn.    The other species of note mentioned below, unless otherwise indicated, will be best accommodated with the Odontoglossums.    There are at present no hybrid Oncidiums.

### Best Species

O. AMPLIATUM has compressed pseudo-bulbs and clear yellow flowers that are borne freely on branching, graceful spikes in

ONCID UM CONCOLOR.

Spring or early Summer.    O. A. MAJUS is finer than the type; it has larger, brighter yellow flowers, and its magnificent spikes are often four feet high—a veritable shower of gold.

O. BRACTEATUM is a strong grower, and has shortly-branched spikes three or four feet high, bearing in Summer an abundance of inch-broad flowers that are bright greenish yellow, spotted with dark purple.

O. CONCOLOR is a small plant, and best grown in suspended pans in the cool house; it has semi-drooping spikes about fifteen inches or more long, with comparatively large light-yellow flowers, the lip being particularly prominent.

O. CRISPUM is a popular and variable species, with rounded flowers of a rich red-brown hue, and yellow markings on the lip, and sometimes also yellow on the margins of the sepals and petals. The spikes are branched, three feet high, and the flowers appear in early Summer.    O. C. GRANDIFLORUM and O. C. CHARLES-WORTHII are splendid forms, with the golden markings highly developed.    Although O. FORBESII and O. GARDNERI are distinct from *O. crispum*, they are nearly allied to it, and have bright brown and yellow flowers in smaller spikes.    All need the same kind of treatment in the cool house.

O. FLEXUOSUM grows well in an intermediate temperature, and is a fine plant for an amateur to cultivate.    Its wiry-stemmed spikes are about a yard high, and the inch-wide flowers are red-brown, barred and tipped with yellow.    Summer is the usual time of flowering.

O. INCURVUM has flowers rather less than an inch across, but these are borne profusely in much-branched, arching spikes that may be six or seven feet long.    They are fragrant, rosy-pink, spotted and tipped with white.    The variety O. I. ALBUM is white, and a somewhat rare plant, and, like the type, it flowers in the Autumn.

O. KRAMERIANUM and O. PAPILIO much resemble each other, and are fairly well known to frequenters of Flower Shows by reason of their large, butterfly-like flowers, borne at the tip of an erect spike. The former has a reddish brown upper sepal and petals, each about two and a half inches long; large, orange-yellow marked lower sepals, and a broad, yellow lip with red-brown marks along its margin. O. PAPILIO has longer upper sepal and petals, red-crimson, red-brown, yellow-barred lower sepals, and a handsome red-bordered lip. In each of these species, as one flower fades the spike elongates slightly, and another bud is produced, and so the plants are never long out of flower. Both must be grown in a warm house.

O. LAMELLIGERUM belongs to the *O. macranthum* group, and has large, brown flowers margined with yellow and with yellow tipped petals.

O. MACRANTHUM is a fine species, and its spikes are often seven or eight feet long. The flowers are three or four inches across, and several of them are borne on each of the branches of the flexuous spike. The upper sepal is yellow and greenish brown, the lower sepals deep yellow, petals brighter yellow, and the lip quite small, white, marked with purple-brown.

O. MARSHALLIANUM is a brilliant and splendid species, with flowers of good size, bright yellow, with red-brown bars and spots on the sepals and petals. The spikes are from three to six feet high, and the flowers are numerous.

O. ORNITHORHYNCHUM has small rosy lilac flowers, carried in branching spikes a couple of feet long. It usually flowers in Winter, as also does its white variety, O. o. ALBUM.

O. PUBES is one of the miniature species, and a pretty plant

ONCIDIUM KRAMERIANUM.

for a suspended pan; it rarely exceeds six inches in height, but its spikes are a foot or more long, drooping, and bear a number of closely set red-brown, yellow marked flowers.

O. PULCHELLUM is a dainty plant that flowers in early Summer; its spikes are rather more than a foot high, and the small flowers are white, charmingly flushed with pink.

O. SARCODES is a showy species, and its spikes, from one to two yards long, are shortly branched and carry a great number of large, yellow-lipped flowers, the sepals and petals being red-brown edged with yellow.

O. SPHACELATUM is another fine species for an amateur to grow. Its flowers are not more than an inch across, but they are produced in large numbers on branched spikes that rise from three to five feet high. The colour is bright red-brown, with bars and tips of golden yellow, the yellow lip having a red-brown mark near its base.

O. SPLENDIDUM is a sturdy, Winter-flowering species; each pseudo-bulb bears a large, stout, leathery leaf, and the spikes rise about two feet high. The flowers are of good size, with a large, flat, yellow lip and greenish yellow, brown-marked sepals and petals.

O. TIGRINUM resembles *O. splendidum*, and bears yellow flowers, margined with red-brown, on branching spikes two or three feet high.

O. VARICOSUM is a beautiful species that flowers in Autumn and Winter. It has nodding spikes two to five feet long, that bear quantities of bright flowers. The sepals and petals are yellow, barred with bright brown, while the golden-yellow lip has a small red-brown stain near the crest. O. VARICOSUM ROGERSII is far more popular than the species, and is altogether larger and finer, the lip often exceeding two inches in width.

Of less value for general purposes, the following have, however, many good points to commend them, and where there is ample room they are worthy of being included in a collection:—
O. ALTISSIMUM, O. AUREUM, O. CANDIDUM (white), O. CARTHA-GINENSE, O. CAVENDISHIANUM (these last two need stove heat), O. CURTUM, O. DASYSTYLE, O. EXCAVATUM, O. JONESIANUM (stove), O. LANCEANUM (stove), O. LIMMINGHEI (a miniature species), O. LOXENSE, O. LURIDUM, O. MONACHICHUM (*O. macranthum* group), O. OLIVACEUM, O. PHALAENOPSIS, O. PRÆTEXTUM, O. PUMILUM, O. SERRATUM (*O. macranthum* group), and O. SUPER-BIENS (*O. macranthum* group).

## PHAIUS

The Phaius are extremely accommodating plants, with one or two exceptions, and there is no good reason why anyone with an ordinary plant stove, or even an intermediate house, should not succeed with many of them, even though not acquainted with Orchids as a class. The terrestrial species have bold leaves about two feet long, and erect spikes rising a yard or so high. The flowers are of good size; the sepals and petals are fairly equal in size and colour, and spread out so as to form, roughly, a semi-circle, with the lower horizontal sepals forming the base line or diameter; the lip is more or less tubular and brightly coloured. The tropical, epiphytal species, *P. Humblotii* and *P. simulans* (or *P. tuberculosus*, as it is still called), need a warm, moist house, and a compost of fibrous peat and sphagnum; the latter has ascending rhizomes, and should be fastened to a piece of tree-fern stem or a teak raft. The terrestrial species are best potted in the Spring,

ODONTOGLOSSUM CRISPUM (ROSE-TINTED VARIETY).

when new growth commences, and if a compost of fibrous peat, loam, and sand is provided, over ample drainage, they will thrive.

### Best Species and Hybrids

P. Blumei, a Javanese species of large growth; flowers olive-brown, with a yellow, crimson-marked lip. P. grandifolius, a fine old species, with spikes three or four feet high; flowers white and chocolate-brown, the lip white and yellow, with crimson veins. P. maculatus, a species that does very well in the cool house; it has green, white-spotted leaves, and spikes of ten or a dozen yellow flowers. P. simulans has pure white sepals and petals, and a large lip, yellow, spotted with crimson, and with a white, purple-marked apex. P. Humbloti is rosy purple, with a broad, red-crimson and yellow lip. P. Wallichii is a strong grower, with spikes four feet high and yellow flowers marked with red-purple.

Very fine hybrids have been raised, chiefly by the late Mr N. C. Cookson. The most notable are P. Chapmanii (*P. Humblotii* x *P. Phœbe*), P. Clive (*P. Cooksoni var. Norman* x *P. simulans*), P. Cooksonæ (*P. grandifolius* x *P. Humblotii*), P. Cooksoni (*P. simulans* x *P. Wallichii*), P. Harold (*P. Cooksoni var. Norman* x *P. Wallichii*), P. Marthæ (*P. Blumei* x *P. simulans*), P. Phœbe (*P. Humblotii* x *P. Wallichii*), P. Ruby (*P. Cooksoni* x *P. Humblotii*, and P. Veitchii (*P. grandifolius* x *P maculatus*).

### Other Species

P. bicolor, P. flavus, P. mishmiensis, and P. pauciflorus.


# PHALÆNOPSIS

The popular species of Phalænopsis are unequalled for grace and beauty by any other Orchids, but there are many that surpass them for gorgeous colouring.   They come from the islands of the East Indies, from the Malayan Archipelago, and some from India, and, with about one exception, need the highest temperature our glass-houses afford, with a continually moist atmosphere.   There is not the slightest doubt that the best way to grow them is to devote a house to them, but where this cannot be done, then the shadiest part of the hottest house should be set apart for their culture.   Teak baskets or cylinders, or broad shallow pans, are the best receptacles, the former for preference, as Phalænopsis appear to like a circulation of moist air about their roots.   Plenty of clean crocks must be provided for drainage, and over this only sphagnum, with a few pieces of crocks added as the moss is worked carefully in among the roots, will be necessary.   A large amount of material is not at all desirable.

Potting is not often necessary, and, indeed, should be only done when absolutely essential, as, for instance, when the plant has quite outgrown its receptacle, or the baskets begin to decay. But a renewal of the sphagnum is desirable each Spring.   The roots of Phalænopsis are fleshy, and adhere closely to the baskets or pans, and delight in coming out from the sphagnum and clinging to the outside of the receptacle; consequently re-potting or re-basketing is no light undertaking, as no matter how careful the operator is, some roots will be broken in the process, and the least carelessness will result in very great damage.   If the roots and receptacle (not the leaves) are soaked for an hour or two in tepid water before potting, the roots may be then more easily detached ; but when pots or pans are used, these should be broken, and the pieces to which roots are firmly attached be allowed to remain.   Spring is the best time to re-pot or renovate the rooting material.   After potting, extra shade must be afforded for some time, and the direct supply of water to the roots must be small.

ONCIDIUM  MARSHALLIANUM.

Although such moisture-loving plants the Phalænopsis dislike being watered overhead, while the drip of cold condensed moisture from the roof on to the plants is disastrous. Phalænopsis are not by any means easily cultivated—that is to say, they are not often found in first-rate condition, but their beauty is such that they warrant every attention and care.

The leaves are flat and fleshy, and they are large in many of the best known kinds. The flowers vary in size, but those of *P. amabilis*, *P. Aphrodite*, and *P. Rimestadiana* are four or five inches across, rounded, and borne in two rows on gracefully arching spikes.

## BEST SPECIES AND HYBIRDS

P. AMABILIS, also known as *P. grandiflora*, is pure white, except for pale yellow and red markings on the lip. P. A. RIME-STADIANA is a beautiful variety that differs from the species only in that it comes from a greater elevation, is more amenable to cultivation, flowers regularly and may be successfully cultivated in an intermediate house or ordinary store. P. APHRODITE, a native of the Philippine Islands, is very like *P. amabilis*, but has a broader purple and yellow-marked lip. P. CASTA is supposed to be a natural hybrid between *P. Aphrodite* and *P. Schilleriana;* the flowers are white, with a light purple flush on the upper sepal and yellow shading on the lower sepals. P. GLORIOSA is very like *P. Aphrodite*, but there are no yellow markings on the lip. P. INTERMEDIA is a natural hybrid between *P. rosea* and *P. Aphrodite*, but it has been also raised artificially. P. VESTA is derived from the same species, *P. rosea* being the pollen parent. The flowers of P. INTERMEDIA are two or three inches across, and produced in the Winter on tall and often branching spikes, particularly in the case of the variety P. I. PORTEI. The white of the sepals and petals is finely contrasted with the deep purple and red of the lip.    P. LEUCORRHODA, a supposed natural hybrid between *P. Aphrodite* and *P. Schilleriana*; flowers white, flushed with purple, and with yellow and purple marks on the lip.    P. ROSEA bears a branched spike about eighteen inches high, and has flowers about an inch and a half across, white, flushed with rosy-purple; lip rosy purple and brown.    P. SANDERIANA, may possibly be a natural hybrid between *P. Aphrodite* and *P. Schilleriana*; it is from the Philippine Islands, and has large rose-pink, white-marked flowers, on spikes about two feet high; lip white, rose, purple and yellow.    P. SCHILLERIANA is very popular, and lends itself to culti- vation better than most species; it sometimes bears branched spikes a yard high, and its large rosy purple flowers are of exquisite beauty.    P. STUARTIANA is a free grower, and has tall branching spikes; its flowers are about two inches across; white, dotted with red-purple on the bases of the segments, the spots being thickest on the yellowish bases of the lower sepals.    P. VEITCHIANA is white, lightly flushed with purple, and with crimson marks on the lip.

There are some very beautiful hybrids, but they are rare plants, in some cases represented by only one specimen, and there fore not to be found catalogued.    These hybrids are essentially plants for the wealthy.    The finest are P. AMESIÆ (*P. amabilis* x *P. intermedia*), P. CASSANDRA (*P. rosea* x *P. Stuartiana*), P. HARRIETÆ (*P. amabilis* x *P. violacea*), P. ROTHSCHILDIANA (*P. amabilis P. Schilleriana*), P. SCHRŒDERÆ (*P. intermedia* x *P· leucorrhoda*), P. SEDENI (*P. amabilis* x *P. Lueddemanniana*), and P. VEITCHÆ (*P. Lueddemanniana* x *P. Sanderiana*).

### OTHER SPECIES

In addition to the foregoing there are several beautiful species, but they have not the attractiveness or the free-flowering

ONC D UM  CR SPUM

habit of those named. These include P. BUYSSONIANA, P. DENTICULATA, P. ESMERALDA, P. LOWII, P. LUEDDEMANNIANA, P. PARISHII, P. SUMATRANA, and P. VIOLACEA, the latter a pretty, small-flowered species with violet-blue flowers. P. LOWII has small purple and white flowers, and is a deciduous species.

## PLATYCLINIS

The elegant little "Chain Orchids" do not form a very large family, nor are they very important, but two species deserve attention where space permits, because they are so distinct and pretty. They are low, slender growers, with tiny pseudo-bulbs, each with a single leaf. The flowers are quite small and indi vidually inconspicuous, but they are produced closely together in a pendulous raceme at the end of a wiry stem. In P. FILIFORMIS the flowers are yellow, the tiny lip being of a deeper shade. In P. GLUMACEA the sweetly hay-scented flowers are greenish white. Both species thrive at the cool end of an intermediate house.

## PLEIONE

The beautiful little "Indian Crocuses," or Pleiones, are charming Orchids that flower in the Winter. They occupy little space, and therefore are to be recommended as suitable for amateurs with small glass accommodation. The plants are deciduous, and flower when leafless. They should be potted as soon as the flowers have faded, and may be separated bulb from bulb, and placed at equal distances apart in broad pans, or be simply potted *en masse*, removing only those new bulbs that stand away from the general group. The compost used should be of peat, loam, sphagnum, and sand, with a layer of sphagnum over the drainage, the latter occupying one-half the depth of the pan. After potting give water through a fine rose, and place the pans on a shelf near the glass in a warm house. No water will then be required for several weeks; indeed, to give water at this season, before new roots have formed and new growth has advanced, is to court failure. When established and growing freely, Pleiones need abundance of water, and may be syringed occasionally, but when the leaves fade, only enough water to keep the bulbs plump will be needed. The flowers are large for the size of the plants, three or four inches across, and they are short-stemmed, so that when a well-grown batch is in bloom, the reason for the popular name is evident.

P. HOOKERIANA has bright rosy-purple flowers, with brown marks and a yellow throat to the lip. P. HUMILIS is blush-white, with blue-purple marks on the fringed lip. These two species grow well in a cool house. P. LAGENARIA is rosy-lilac, and has a very handsome lip, white, marked with crimson, purple, red, and yellow. P. MACULATA, pure white, with a yellow throat and yellow marks on the lip, is a lovely Orchid that flowers at the end of the year. P. PRÆCOX is rosy purple, with yellow marks on the pale rose or white lip.


## RENANTHERA

For a long number of years the old RENANTHERA COCCINEA was the only species in cultivation, and though it is remarkable as well as brilliantly beautiful when in flower, it grows to such an enormous length that only in very high stoves can it be accommodated. And usually it is only when a plant is allowed to grow to the height of a dozen feet or more that it flowers well. It some-

SOBRALIA VEITCHII.

times blooms at five or six feet high, but as a general rule its long, scandent habit puts it out of court as a popular Orchid. The flowers have deep crimson, yellow-spotted petals and upper sepal, and the large lower sepals are vermilion, the lip being red and yellow. These brilliant blooms, three inches across, are borne in large numbers on a large, branched raceme. R. STOREYI is like *R. coccinea* in general habit and appearance, but the flowers are crimson and orange, with yellow and white marks on the crimson lip. By far the best species for general cultivation, and one that has now placed the genus in a foremost horticultural position, is R. IMSCHOOTIANA. This Burmese species is from six inches to two feet high, and its branching, graceful spikes carry (in good specimens), a score or more of brilliant vermilion flowers. All the species have Vanda-like leaves and growth, and need the same treatment as the Vandas that are grown in the stove.


## SOBRALIA

The tall, slender, reedy growths, and large handsome flowers of the Sobralias are familiar to most horticulturists. The species and hybrids are easily grown in an intermediate house or ordinary plant stove, in pots, in a mixture of peat and fibrous loam, with some sphagnum and sand added. Plenty of water, overhead syringing, and liquid manure in the case of established specimens, should be afforded when the plants are in full growth, but afterwards much less water will suffice, although, as the plants are evergreen, they must never be allowed to get quite dry at the roots, or the leaves will fall and the plants be severely harmed. In many instances the flowers are as large as those of the finest Cattleyas, and equally attractive, but the Sobralias have one fault, which is that the flowers are of short duration.   This is compensated for by a succession of flowers from the same stem.

### BEST SPECIES AND HYBRIDS

S. LEUCOXANTHA, white, with large, golden yellow, orange throated lip.   S. LUCASIANA, white, rose-tinted, with rose-purple, yellow throated lip.   S. MACRANTHA, very free, rich purple, with white, yellow marked throat.   S. M. KEINASTIANA is pure white. S. SANDERIANA is white, rose tinted, with crimson-purple, yellow throated lip.   S. VIRGINALIS, white, flushed with rose, yellow throat.   S. XANTHOLEUCA, light yellow, with deep yellow lip; a great beauty.

The best hybrids are S. AMESIANA (*S. xantholeuca* x *S. Wilsoniana*), S. VEITCHII (*S. macrantha* x *S. xantholeuca*).

### OTHER SPECIES

S. CATTLEYA, very tall, seldom flowers; S. DECORA, S. LOWII, S. SESSILIS, and S. WILSONIANA.

### SOPHRO-CATTLEYA

A small but increasing family of hybrids between Sophronitis and Cattleya.   They are of dwarf, neat habit, and the shapely flowers are usually of brilliant colour.   Cattleya treatment seems to suit them.   The best are S.-c. BATEMANIANA (*C. intermedia* x *S. grandiflora*), S.-c. CALYPSO (*C. Loddigesii* x *S. grandiflora*), S.-c. CHAMBERLAINII (*C. Harrisoniana* x *S. grandiflora*), S.-c. EXIMIA (*C. Bowringiana* x *S. grandiflora*), S.-c. HARDYANA (*C. Acklandiæ* x *S. grandiflora*), S.-c. IMPERATRIX (*C. Mossiæ* x *S. grandiflora*), and S.-c. SAXA (*C. Trianæ* x *S. grandiflora*).

## SOPHRO-LÆLIA

The best of the hybrids between Lælia and Sophronitis are— S.-L. LÆTA (*L. Dayana* x *S. grandiflora*), S.-L. MARRIOTTII (*L. flava* x *S. grandiflora*), and S.-C. ORPETI (*L. pumila* x *S. grandiflora*).

## SOPHRONITIS

One of the most delightful of the small growing Orchids is the brilliant scarlet SOPHRONITIS GRANDIFLORA, a species that has been used as a parent in the production of many bigeneric hybrids. It is only three inches high, and it grows well in shallow pans, in peat, broken leaves and sphagnum, suspended at the warmest end of the cool house, and treated like an Odontoglossum. It flowers with great freedom in the Winter, and as each flower is nearly three inches across, and of a beautiful shade of rich scarlet, with orange marks on the lip, it is a most effective little plant, and just the one for amateurs to cultivate. There are other species—S. CERNUA and S. VIOLACEA—but they have small claim to cultivation compared with S. GRANDIFLORA.

## THUNIA

So remarkably beautiful and graceful are the Thunias, that the wonder is they are not more regularly grown in our glass houses, especially as they can be cultivated with ease by anyone who can manage a deciduous, tropical bulbous plant. The Thunias grow about two or three feet high, and have light coloured stems and leaves.   They flower at the ends of the new growth, and after flowering, soon begin to lose their leaves and go to rest.   Plenty of heat and moisture are desirable when the plants are in full growth, and if they are well rooted they may be given weak liquid manure also.   When at rest, a cooler house will suit them, and no water will be needed after all the leaves have fallen until the following Spring, when new growth begins to push from the base of the old stems.   This is the time to re-pot. Water sparingly until the new roots have taken possession of the new material.

### Best Species and Hybrids

S. ALBA, white, with five raised, fringed, purple lines on the lip.   S. BENSONIÆ, bright, rich purple, with yellow, fringed lines on the lip.   S. BRYMERIANA, white, with crimson marks and yellow, fringed lines on the lip.   S. MARSHALLIÆ, white, with lip beautifully marked with yellow and orange.   S. VEITCHII is a fine hybrid between *S. Marshalliæ* and *S. Bensoniæ*.

## VANDA

With a few exceptions the Vandas have lost the popularity they once possessed.   A quarter of a century or more ago they were grown largely in all extensive collections of indoor plants, and great pains were taken to produce fine specimens.   Even when not in flower the stronger growing Vandas are bold, handsome plants, with large, channelled leaves, borne in two ranks on stout erect stems.   The flowers vary a great deal in size and appearance.   *V. Amesiana* has small, whitish flowers, while *V. San-*

VANDA CŒRULEA.

*deriana* has flat flowers five inches broad. The latter has stout, large leaves, while *V. Hookeriana* has slender terete leaves.

Most of the Vandas require a high temperature and a moist atmosphere, but when new leaves cease to form for the season, and the tips of the roots become sealed over, a much reduced water supply will suffice, although, as the species are all evergreen, absolutely dry conditions at the roots must not be permitted. Potting should be done only when the condition of the rooting material or the increased size of the plant renders such an operation imperative. The new year is the best time for re-potting, and if this is not necessary the surface of the rooting material should be removed and new sphagnum given. In the course of time Vandas lose some of their lower leaves and become " leggy "; when this is the case, the lower part of the stem and roots should be cut away, as there will be plenty of roots from the part of the stem above the pot to carry the plant well after re-potting.

The roots are brittle, and great care must be taken to prevent injury to them. It is a good plan to crock the pots two-thirds of their depth, inserting a stout stick as the crocks are placed in position, for the purpose of keeping the plant upright and secure. Then place a layer of sphagnum over the drainage, and carefully work the roots of the plant into the pot. Fill in among the roots with smaller, clean crocks, to within an inch or so of the rim of the pot, and finish off with a thick layer of live sphagnum, slightly mounded up to the stem of the plant. A good watering with tepid water should follow potting, and shade from sunshine must be afforded until the plants have re-established themselves. It should, however, be remembered that Vandas do not require the heavy shading that Aerides do. From March to the end of October the temperature should range from 65 to 70 degrees at night to from 70 to 85 or 90 degrees by day, according to the weather outside.   For the rest of the year a minimum of 60 degrees should be secured by fire heat.

*Vanda cærulea*, the most popular species, does not do well under the tropical conditions indicated, but is best managed in an intermediate house, where plenty of ventilation is provided on all favourable occasions; it has usually been kept much too hot, and too wet at the roots while at rest.

### BEST SPECIES

V. AMESIANA is a dwarf grower, and has a long spike of white flowers that are usually prettily tinted with blush, and have a deep reddish rose lip; the flowers are small, produced in late Spring or early Summer.

V. CŒRULEA is a lovely Orchid with stiff spikes of rounded, blue flowers; the flowers vary in the depth of their blue colouring, some being of a wonderfully deep and rich shade, and measuring as much as four or five inches across.   As many as ten to fifteen flowers may be carried on a spike.

V. INSIGNIS has rounded, fleshy flowers; white, light brown, and buff, spotted with red-brown.   In general appearance this species resembles *V. tricolor.*

V. KIMBALLIANA is of slender growth, and bears nodding spikes of charming flowers.   The individual blooms are white, suffused with rose, and with a yellowish, purple-spotted lip. They are about two inches across, and ten or a dozen are carried on a spike.

V. LAMELLATA is dwarf, and flowers freely, its white, brown, and magenta-purple flowers appearing, a dozen or twenty together, in the Winter, on a spike about eighteen inches long.   V. L. BOXALLII is larger and brighter than the type.

VANDA SANDERANA.

V. PARISHII grows like a Phalænopsis, and has large fleshy flowers with greenish yellow colouring and red spots, and a white and violet-purple lip.

V. SANDERIANA is a grand species, but it is by no means an easy one to grow. It does best in a basket or cylinder in the hottest house, and when it produces its big blooms, several together on a short spike, it is magnificent. The upper sepal is rose and white, the lower sepals tawny yellow, reticulately veined with rose-red. The petals are rose and white, and the small lip is yellow, heavily marked with red and purple.

V. SUAVIS is an old and popular species of large growth, and a good stem often bears two spikes of large, fragrant flowers. The sepals are white, freely marked with red-purple; the petals are similarly coloured, and the lip is rich rose-purple. V. s. GOTSCHALKEI, V. s. ROLLISONI, and V. s. VEITCHII are fine varieties of this useful species.

V. TERES is a lovely plant, and one that flowers freely in the early Spring when well managed. It does best at the warm end of a stove, where it receives all possible sunshine and can be syringed freely when growing. It should be planted in crocks and sphagnum. The growth is slender, and the leaves erect and terete. The spikes carry three or four flowers, each three or four inches across. The sepals are white, more or less suffused with rose; the broader petals are deep rose, or purple-rose; and the large lip yellow, rose, and red. There are several distinct varieties, V. T. CANDIDA having white flowers with yellow and rose markings on the lip.

V. TRICOLOR is very like *V. suavis;* its flowers are about three inches across, yellowish white, with red-brown marks, and a white, purple, and red-brown lip. V. T. INSIGNIS, V. T. PLANI-LABRIS, and V. T. PATERSONI are well-marked varieties.

## OTHER SPECIES

Other species of more or less interest and value are V. BENSONI, V. CŒRULESCENS, V. CONCOLOR, V. CRISTATA, V. HOOKERIANA, V. LIMBATA, and V. ROXBURGHII.

## ZYGOCOLAX

This is a small group of beautiful little hybrids between the small growing *Colax jugosus* and species of *Zygopetalum*. They have greenish brown marks on the sepals and petals, and a fleshy lip usually with blue or violet-purple colouring. The principal kinds are Z.-C. AMESIANUS (*C. jugosus* x *Z. Mackayi*), Z.-C. LEOPARDINUS (*C. jugosus* x *Z. maxillare*), Z.-C. VEITCHII (*C. jugosus* x *Z. crinitum*), and Z.-C. WIGANIANUS (*C. jugosus* x *Z. intermedium*).

## ZYGOPETALUM

The best of the Zygopetalums form a group of attractive, easily grown, and extremely useful Orchids. They are of sturdy growth, with stout pseudo-bulbs and fairly large, green leaves. In some of them the rhizomes are elongated, and these should be placed in pots, but be given a piece of old tree-fern stem to grow and root upon. Fibrous peat and loam, with a little sphagnum and sand added, make a suitable compost. During the late Autumn and Winter the several species should be placed in an intermediate house, but throughout the Summer the cool house is the best place for them. As they are evergreen, the plants do not require a severe rest, nor must they ever be allowed to get dry at the roots, but, obviously, much less water is needed when growth is finished for

GROUP OF SOBRALIAS.

the year than at other times.   Thrips sometimes attack the foliage, and a sharp lookout must be kept for them, or the leaves will soon be disfigured and the vitality of the plant impaired.

## Best Species and Hybrids

Z. CRINITUM flowers in late Winter or Spring, and is about eighteen inches high.   Several flowers are carried on the erect two-feet spikes, and individually they are about three inches across. The sepals and  petals are green with brown bars; lip white, heavily veined with violet-blue or red-purple.

Z. INTERMEDIUM is a very fine garden plant, and every amateur who takes up Orchid culture should obtain it.   The green sepals and petals are shaded with brown, and the large lip is white, with radiating lines of deep violet or purple.

Z. MACKAYI is a fine species, with yellowish green sepals and petals marked with purple-brown; lip white, with radiating marks of violet-purple.   Flowers about three inches across, and fragrant.

Z. MAXILLARE is scarcely so tall as the species already named. Its flowers are about two and a half inches across; sepals and petals green, marked with red-brown; lip deep violet-blue, shading to pale blue or white at the margin.   Z. M. GAUTIERI has rather larger flowers, with deep purple colouring.

The best hybrids are Z. CLAYI (*Z. crinitum* x *Z. maxillare*), Z. PERRENOUDI (*Z. intermedium* x *Z. maxillare*), Z. SANDERI (*Z. Mackayi* x *Z.Perrenoudi*), and Z. SEDENI (*Z. Mackayi* x *Z. maxillare*).

# ORCHIDS OF LESSER VALUE

## ACACALLIS

THE only member of this small genus to which any reference need be made in this work is *Acacallis cyanea*, a dwarf plant from Brazil, and closely allied to the Vandas. It has blue flowers that bear a resemblance to those of a small Odontoglossum. It has a creeping habit of growth, and should be grown on a block of wood or an upright teak raft, with a little peat fibre and sphagnum about its roots. This rare and beautiful little Orchid, often described as Aganisia cœrulea, must be grown in the high temperature and moist atmosphere of a stove.

## ACANTHOPHIPPIUM

Most members of this genus of terrestrial Orchids are natives of Tropical Asia, and therefore need abundance of heat and moisture during the greater part of the year, but during the Winter water must be withheld, except through the medium of the atmosphere. The erect spikes carry from three to seven fairly large, fleshy flowers, but these are not very effective. The principal species are A. BICOLOR, yellow and purple; A. CURTISII, purple-rose, yellow, and white; A. JAVANICUM, yellow and purple; A. STRIATUM, white and red; and A. SYLHETENSE, creamy white, and purple.

ZYGOPETALUM CRINITUM.

## ACINETA

·An interesting genus of epiphytal Orchids from Tropical America. They have drooping spikes of flowers, and as these proceed from the base of the pseudo-bulb, the plants should be grown in baskets suspended from the roof in a stove. Although evergreen, these Orchids require hardly any water when not making new growth, but they can hardly be over-watered when growing freely, if planted in a mixture of peat and sphagnum. Their requirements are practically the same as those of Stanhopeas. The flowers are fleshy and fragrant, and there may be as many as a dozen on a spike. Among the several species those of most importance are A. BARKERI, golden yellow lip, spotted with red; A. DENSA, yellow, marked with crimson and red ; A. HRUBYANA, white and purple; and A. HUMBOLDTII, chocolate-purple and rose.

## AGANISIA

AGANISIA IONOPTERA and A. LEPIDA are two pretty little Orchids that will succeed with the Angræcums. They are both from Tropical America, and the former has white, violet-marked flowers, while A. LEPIDA has white flowers, marked with chocolate and purple.

## ANCISTROCHILUS

The pretty little Orchid, so long known as *Pachystoma Thomsoniana*, is now referred to ANCISTROCHILUS THOMSONIANUS. It is a native of West Tropical Africa, and comparatively rare in cultivation. The plant is of lowly growth, about six inches high, with slightly taller spikes of rather large, white flowers, with a bright purple-marked lip. Peat, sphagnum, and broken leaves form a suitable potting mixture. The warmest house, careful watering, and a period of decided rest should be afforded, as well as a light position. The flowering time is October and November.

## ANŒCTOCHILUS

Many a clever grower has come to grief over the little group of Orchids known generally as Anœctochilus. These are not cultivated for the beauty of their flowers, but for their exquisitely beautiful foliage. The leaves are not large; they range from two to four inches in length, and from one to three inches in breadth; but the various combinations of shades of green, and the charming veinings and markings of silver and gold, copper and red, bronze and grey, are so indescribably lovely, that most Orchid lovers take up the culture of Anœctochilus at some time or other, and usually with a small degree of success. The curious part about their culture is that they may be beautiful one season and almost a failure the next, even when the conditions appear to have been identical. Being difficult to import and cultivate, they are rather expensive plants, small specimens only of one or two of the most tractable kinds costing 5s. each, while many of the others are several guineas each.

The most successful method of dealing with these little gems is to grow them in the warmest house, give them plenty of shade, and cover them with a bell glass. Small pots or shallow pans are the best receptacles, and these must be amply drained. Sphagnum, finely broken crocks, sand, and a little peat fibre, make up a suitable potting mixture, and this must be kept moist at all seasons of the year, although when the plants cease to make fresh growth, less moisture will suffice than at other seasons.

Two good Anœctochilus are A. CONCINNUS, olive-green with reddish veins, and A. REGALIS, dark bronzy-green with gold veins. The two members of this group most easily managed are HÆMARIA DAWSONIANA (*Anœctochilus Dawsonianus*), and MACODES PETOLA (*Anœctochilus Petolus*); the former has rich green leaves, shaded with olive, and beautifully marked with bright copper-coloured veins; and the latter has broad olive-green leaves, exquisitely veined with bright yellow. Other beautiful things are DOSSINIA MARMORATA (*Annœtochilus Lowii*), GOODYERA PICTA, G. ROLLISSONI, ANŒCTOCHILUS SANDERIANUS and A. SETACEUS. But there are many others of almost equal beauty that may be obtained when a fair amount of success has inspired the cultivator and given him sufficient confidence to warrant their purchase.

## ANSELLIA

Where there is a stove or East Indian House one or more Ansellias should be cultivated, because few plants grown in such heated structures are so noble or so free flowering. The various species are chiefly from Tropical Africa, and grow from two feet to four feet high. As their flowering season under cultivation is Winter, and usually January, their usefulness is great, especially when it is remembered that the drooping, branching spikes of *A. africana* carry from thirty to a hundred flowers. All the species root freely, and in the case of established plants the roots often rise above the compost, and make quite a little thicket on top of the pot. It is necessary, therefore, to provide pots of good size, in proportion to the plant, and a compost of fibrous peat, fibrous loam, some dry, broken leaves and sand, over good drainage. Potting is best done soon after the flowers have faded, as new growth commences at this period and new roots appear.    Abundance of moisture in the atmosphere and at the roots is necessary for the full development of the tall growths, but for a little while after potting the supply at the roots must be quite moderate, and when the growths cease to extend and do not produce new leaves, this must be taken as a sign that the plant needs a rest.    A severely restricted supply of water will suffice from this time until the spikes are advancing.    Water must not be allowed to collect in the centre or heart of the new growth, or damping may follow.

The best species is ANSELLIA AFRICANA, which has a yellow lip, and yellow sepals and petals, spotted and barred with red-brown.    A. CONFUSA has clusters of small, light yellow flowers. A. CONGOENSIS is rather dwarfer than the rest, and has the white side lobes of its lip marked with brown; A. GIGANTEA closely resembles A. AFRICANA, but differs in having larger flowers and producing these in upright spikes.    Ansellias produce their spikes from the top of the growths.


## ARACHNANTHE

The Arachnanthes are closely allied to the Vandas, and need similar general treatment to that found successful for the tropical members of the latter genus.    They are not often seen in modern collections, but when A. CATHCARTII and A. LOWII are well grown, and in flower, few Orchids attract so much attention. A. CATHCARTII comes from the deep, hot, moist valleys of the Eastern Himalaya.    Its fleshy flowers, three inches across, are borne four or five together on short stiff spikes.    The under side

of the flower is whitish, and the white lip is streaked with red, while the rounded sepals and petals are tawny yellow, banded with red in such a way as to suggest the lines of a cobweb, and this fanciful suggestion led to the generic title of Arachnanthe. Another wonderful species is A. LOWII, a native of the coastal forests of the Bornean province of Sarawak. It has flexuous spikes from two feet to twelve feet long, and while the basal pair of flowers on each spike are yellow, spotted with red-purple, all the others (and there may be thirty or forty of them), are greenish yellow, heavily and irregularly blotched with rich chocolate-red. A. CATHCARTII requires some support, and should be placed in a pot or pan with a teak raft up which it may climb, and round which it may twine its roots. Other interesting species are A. CLARKEI and A. MOSCHIFERA. Many of the species have been classed as Vandas and some as Esmeraldas.


## ARUNDINA

The Arundinas are graceful, tall, terrestrial Orchids, very much like, and succeeding under the same conditions as, the Sobralias. They have beautiful, rosy flowers, with white and yellow marks on the lip, but the plants take up a great deal of room, and are seldom effective or useful for general culture. A. BAMBUSÆFOLIA and A. PHILIPPINENSIS are the principal species.


## ASPASIA

A foot or less in height, ASPASIA LUNATA produces its green and white, brown-spotted flowers in racemes, during early spring. It is a pretty little Orchid that an amateur might well take some trouble with, and it may be successfully grown with and like the Miltonias. A. PRINCIPISSA is taller than the foregoing, and has brown flowers, with a white, purple marked lip.


## BARTHOLINA

One of the most beautiful of South African terrestrial Orchids is BARTHOLINA PECTINATA, but unfortunately it is expensive, as the price is about a guinea and a half. The manner of growth is interesting; there is a tuberous root, and from this stock rises one leaf, and an erect flower spike that carries at its apex a single bloom. The chief feature of the flower is its large, fimbriated, violet, green shaded lip. The comparatively small sepals and petals are white, with violet shading. It may be grown in a cool greenhouse or frame, in pots, in a mixture of light loam, leaf mould and sand.


## BATEMANNIA

The pretty BATEMANNIA COLLEYI will appeal strongly to those whose taste is not wholly on the side of large and showy flowers. It has short, square, furrowed pseudo-bulbs, and ribbed, deep green leaves. In the Spring it produces short spikes of flowers, these being purple-brown and green on the sepals and petals, and white with red marks on the lip. The whole plant rarely exceeds eight inches in height, and grows best in sphagnum with a little peat added. The best position for it is a shady place in the Cattleya House or Intermediate House. An endeavour should be made to always keep the roots just moist and to avoid over-watering. BATEMANNIA COLLEYI commemorates a great lover of Orchids, the late Mr J. Bateman and his collector, Mr Colley, who found the species in British Guiana in 1837.


## BIFRENARIA

This Brazilian genus is closely allied to Maxillaria, and, from a horticultural point of view, differs chiefly in sometimes producing its flowers in pairs instead of singly.    The plants should be grown in pans or baskets, in peat and sphagnum, and under the same conditions as the Maxillarias, always remembering to give water sparingly when they are not in active growth.    The best and most popular species, and one that often finds a place in an ordinary plant stove, is BIFRENARIA HARRISONIÆ.    This has fleshy, fragrant flowers, creamy white or pale yellow, with a purple, yellow-marked lip; the colour varies somewhat, and a few varieties have been given distinctive names.    B. HARRISONIÆ usually flowers in the Spring, while B. AURANTIACA, which has yellow, orange-spotted flowers, blooms in the Autumn.    Other species sometimes grown are B. TYRIANTHINA, with purple flowers, and B. VITELLINA, with yellow flowers.


## BLETIA

The Bletias are easily grown cool-house Orchids, but they do not find much favour with growers.    The best species is B. HYA-CINTHINA, one that is practically hardy in the warmer parts of England and Ireland.    It has long, plicate, handsome, green leaves, and carries its deep rose-purple flowers on slender spikes. B. SHEPHERDII is more robust, growing three feet high and bearing fair sized red-purple flowers, in which the lip is lined with yellow.

As the latter species is from Jamaica, it requires warmer conditions than B. HYACINTHINA; the warmest end of the Odontoglossum House will suit it.   The genus is of interest from the fact that the first exotic Orchid introduced into British gardens was B. VERE-CUNDA, collected in the Bahamas by Peter Collinson, in 1731, and flowered in England in 1732.

## BOLLEA

Only one species calls for attention, *i.e.* BOLLEA CŒLESTIS, a Colombian Orchid requiring a moist, shady position in a warm house, a mixture of peat and sphagnum to root in, and amply drained pans or baskets.   It grows about a foot or fifteen inches high, and bears its flowers on stiff spikes that are about as tall as the leaves.   There is usually one flower on a spike, and it is three or four inches across, violet-blue, with yellow lines on the lip. A rarely grown, but pretty, Summer flowering Orchid.   B. LA LINDEI, B. LAWRENCEANUM, and B. PATINI are of interest to those who like uncommon Orchids.   All the Bolleas are without pseudo-bulbs, and are frequently described as Zygopetalums.

## BROUGHTONIA

The Jamaican BROUGHTONIA SANGUINEA was sent to Kew as long ago as 1793.   It is a small plant, with flattish pseudo-bulbs, and slender, branched, arching spikes of deep red flowers that are small, but of an unusual shade of colour.   It is best managed by being grown in a shallow teak basket or on a raft, with very little sphagnum and peat about its roots, and suspended in the Cattleya House.   While "resting," it needs very little water, but must be

CATTLEYA TRIANÆ

given an ample supply at other seasons.    It loves plenty of light, and only needs shade from the hottest mid-day sun.

## BULBOPHYLLUM

In the "Kew Hand-list of Orchids," dated 1904, no fewer than seventy species of Bulbophyllums are cited as being in cultivation in the Kew collection, but the extent of the genus is no indication of its popularity or its horticultural value.    To the botanist and the lover of the curious the many species appeal very strongly, but most florists, gardeners, and nurserymen regard them as some of the "weeds" of the great Orchid family.    The genus is widely spread, and species are found in such widely separated regions as the Malay, Central America, Africa and Australasia. It is difficult to treat on such a large genus in a general way, but it has been found that the great majority of species thrive in peat and sphagnum, in pans or baskets, and love plenty of heat and moisture when growing freely, but need much less moisture and slightly cooler conditions when "resting."    Most of the species are evergreen, but a few, like *Bulbophyllum comosum*, are deciduous.

B. BARBIGERUM is a tiny plant with little spikes of dull purple flowers, each of which is furnished with an articulate lip that carries a tuft of silky hairs, and oscillates in a peculiar, jerky manner, with every movement of the air; B. COMOSUM produces dense, decurved, brush-like spikes of whitish, hay-scented flowers; B. ERICSSONII carries its large, yellowish-white flowers in an umbellate cluster; B. GRANDIFLORUM is the largest flowered member of the genus, its upper sepal often measuring nearly five

M

inches long and two inches across, dull greenish yellow with white spots; B. LOBBI is bright yellow, veined with purple, and its lip is so beautifully articulated that it swings backward and forward at the slightest movement; B. DEARII and the Siamese variety of B. LOBBII have a similar lip.


## CALOPOGON

Only one species calls for attention, and it is the pretty CALOPOGON PULCHELLUS, a North American plant introduced in 1771. It has tuberous roots, and may be successfully cultivated in a cold frame, in a mixture of peat, loam, and sphagnum. It is hardy in favoured situations, but when planted out of doors it should have some protecting material, such as bracken or ashes, placed over it during the Winter. The species grows about eighteen inches high, and produces its purples flowers on tall, slender spikes in the Summer.


## CALYPSO

A very interesting hardy terrestrial Orchid is CALYPSO BORE-ALIS. This rarely grows more than six inches high, and its curious rose and brown-coloured flowers are produced early in the season. Grown in sandy peat and loam, in a moist frame, away from direct sunshine, and only protected in the Winter and during severe storms, it is a source of great pleasure. The root is tuberous, and propagation is by means of off-sets or divisions.

## CAMARIDIUM

The few species belonging to this genus of stove Orchids come from Tropical America, but CAMARIDIUM OCHROLEUCUM is only occasionally cultivated. It has white flowers and usually blooms in the Winter, and should be grown in shallow, well-drained pans or baskets of peat and sphagnum, the crown of the plant being kept well above the compost.

## CAMAROTIS

Half a century ago or more CAMAROTIS PURPUREUS was highly esteemed among lovers of Orchids, and it is on record that a plant exhibited from the Westonbirt collection in 1850 carried no fewer than one hundred spikes of rosy flowers, the deep rose-purple lip adding to the colour effect. This plant is not often met with now, but probably its popularity would return if some one presented it in first-rate condition. A high temperature and abundance of moisture at all times suits it best, while sphagnum and broken crocks suffice as a rooting medium.

## CATASETUM

Although Catasetums are among the most remarkable and interesting Orchids, and invariably attract a great deal of attention when exhibited, most people are well content to let some one else do the growing. Catasetums are of little horticultural value, and before it was known that the male and female flowers differed in structure and colour, and were usually borne on separate spikes, the nomenclature of the genus was confused.   The male flowers are the most prominent, and in most cases there is a spring-like arrangement consisting of a curved horn-like attachment to the column, which, when released by an intruding insect, forcibly ejects the adhesive pollen masses.   The writer well remembers an inquisitive old lady receiving the pollen masses of *Catasetum macro-carpum* on the tip of her nose as a result of a too close inspection of a plant on view at Kew.   As the adhesive matter congeals rapidly, the discomfiture of the lady caused some amusement for a few moments.

Catasetums are not difficult to cultivate, provided a position in the stove is afforded them where they will receive abundance of moisture at the roots and in the atmosphere while growing freely, and also strong light.   When the new growths cease to form new leaves, the plants should be placed so as to receive full sunshine, and at the same time the supply of water at the roots must be steadily reduced, until, when the leaves turn yellow and fall, it is withheld altogether, and the compost is allowed to remain dry during the resting period.   When the flower spikes appear a little water will be needed, but it must be given sparingly until after the plants have been re-potted, and new roots and growth make larger demands.   Catasetums should be re-potted annually, or rather, should be given new rooting material each year.   Teak baskets are better receptacles than pots or pans, as they are the more readily suspended near the roof.   The compost found most suit-able for these Orchids consists of peat and sphagnum in equal proportions, with small crocks, sand, and broken charcoal added. When at rest, place the plants in a light position in the stove, either on a shelf or raised above the moisture-holding material on the stage.

The most desirable species are C. BUNGEROTHII, which has

large, pure white flowers; there are finely coloured varieties of (or hybrids from) it, introduced by M. Linden some years ago, *i.e.*, MIRABILE, LINDENII, and IMPERIALE; C. MACROCARPUM, with flowers often nearly four inches across, yellowish, spotted with purple; C. RODIGASIANUM, green and purple-brown; and C. TABULARE, green or green and white.

## CHONDRORHYNCHA

This small Colombian genus contains one charming little plant that is but rarely cultivated with success.    A stove or inter-mediate temperature appears to suit it best, with peat and sphagnum as a rooting medium.    The flowers of CHONDRORHYNCHA CHESTER-TONII are large for the size of the plant, and remarkable for the beautifully fimbriated margin of the broad lip.    The colour is yellow.    Two other species are in cultivation, *i.e.*, C. FIMBRIATA, sulphur-yellow with brown spots, and C. LENDYANA, pale yellow.

## CIRRHOPETALUM.

This is a large genus of quaint and interesting Orchids, found widely distributed throughout the Eastern Tropics.    Akin to the Bulbophyllums in many ways, they will thrive under the same cultural conditions.    Very few of them are of horticultural value, and it is only in the great national collections, like those at Kew and Glasnevin, or a private collection like Sir Trevor Lawrence's, that they are seen in quantity.    In most species the two lower sepals are enlarged and extended into slender tails, and form the chief attraction, while the lip is often very small, but so daintily poised that it is set wagging by the slightest movement of the flower.   Dr Lindley considered that the wagging lip and quaintly curious appearance of the flowers of *Cirrhopetalum chinense* gave to the Chinese the idea for those comical figures of men and women with wagging heads, tongues, and chins, with which we are all familiar.   The writer's selection from the many species consists of C. APPENDICULATUM, C. COLLETTII, C. FIMBRIATUM, C. ORNA-TISSIMUM, C. PICTURATUM, C. CUMINGII, C. ROBUSTUM, C. ROTHS-CHILDEANUM, and C. ROXBURGHII.   The elegant little flowers are borne in umbels at the end of a slender spike that rises only a few inches high, and the arrangement is such as to suggest a tiny Japanese parasol for a diminutive fairy.


## COLAX.

There are several members of this Brazilian genus, but only one is at all popular.   COLAX JUGOSUS is very interesting; it grows about a foot or less in height, and carries two or three of its effective flowers on a stiff spike.   The blooms usually appear in the early Summer, and they are two inches in diameter, with white or cream sepals, white purple-blotched petals, and a fleshy, white lip that is also streaked, splashed, and spotted with deep purple. Potted in peat and sphagnum, with the addition of sand and broken leaves, it roots freely if placed in a shady position in the Cool House, or at the coolest end of the Cattleya House. The foliage should not be wetted, as it is subject to spot, and when the plant is resting, only enough water should be given to keep the pseudo-bulbs plump.

The great interest that centres round this Orchid is due to the fact that, though always regarded as closely allied to the Lycastes and the Maxillarias, it has proved to be very nearly related to the Zygopetalums, for it has wedded freely with the latter.    The result of this association is seen in the series of beautiful little bigeneric Orchids referred to under the title of ZYGOCOLAX (which see).

## CORYANTHES

Though of little value horticulturally, the Coryanthes show a floral development of so remarkable a character that they occupy a high position among the marvels of the vegetable kingdom.    A minute description of the flower would occupy considerable space, and would not convey a very good idea of its extraordinary shape. It must suffice to say that the flowers are large and fleshy, short-lived, and have a lip that hangs from a stout, hooded arm, and is broadly pouched so as to catch the nectar dripping from two finger-like processes.    The chief species are CORYANTHES MACRANTHA and C. MACULATA.    The former is yellow and red, and the latter yellow, crimson and purple.    They are best grown as advised for Stanhopeas, except that they must not be dried so severely during their resting season.

## COMPARETTIA

The Comparettias are lowly Orchids with long-spurred, showy flowers, borne in slender, drooping racemes.    They grow best in baskets in peat and sphagnum, suspended in a shady part of the Cattleya House, or in the Intermediate House.    COMPARETTIA MACROPLECTON is the best species, as it flowers freely, producing its rose, purple-speckled flowers in the Summer.    The lip is very large compared with the other segments.    Other species, seldom grown, are C. COCCINEA, scarlet and orange; C. FALCATA, crimson-purple; and C. SPECIOSA, orange-red.


## CYCNOCHES

The species of Cycnoches are very interesting, but they are not beautiful or generally useful. Where there is ample space for them, a few plants should be grown because of the curious structure of the flowers. The male and female flowers differ considerably in form, as in the case of Catasetums, and the cultural treatment found suitable for the latter genus is applicable to the Cycnoches. A stove temperature, a liberal supply of water during the season of vigorous growth, practically no water while resting (the leaves are deciduous), and a compost of fibrous peat and broken leaves, are the chief points to be considered. When at rest the plants are best kept in a light position at the coolest end of the stove. CYCNOCHES CHLOROCHILON is the species most extensively cultivated; it has large, fleshy flowers of a bright yellow-green colour, and as these are produced in Summer, they are seen frequently at exhibitions. C. PENTADACTYLON has smaller, yellow-green flowers that are prettily blotched with brown. C. CHLOROCHILON is popularly known as the Swan Orchid.


## CYRTOPODIUM

For some unaccountable reason the several species of Cyrto-podium have never been popular, and yet it is difficult to conceive more effective plants than these are when well managed. The chief difficulty is that they are all tall growers, and consequently it is not in every garden there is a stove-house high enough to accommodate them easily. In former years, when large stove plants were popular, and there were fairly high houses for their accommodation, the case was different. The Cyrtopodiums offer a fine opportunity for the display of horticultural skill in gardens where the conveniences permit. Their chief requirements are plenty of root room, ample drainage, a compost of equal parts of fibrous loam and old manure, a high stove temperature, and an abundance of water when growth is vigorous. All the species are deciduous, and while at rest they may with advantage be placed with the Cattleyas and given no water until new growth commences. Anyone who can grow the splendid deciduous Caladiums well should find no difficulty in cultivating Cyrtopodiums to perfection.

The principal species are C. ALICIÆ, a Brazilian species that has rather small, yellow-green, brown-spotted flowers, in branching spikes, and its numerous bracts of similar colour add considerably to its effectiveness; C. ANDERSONI, from the West Indies, grows five feet high, and produces an abundance of bright yellow flowers on a yard-high, branched spike, in early Summer ; C. PUNCTATUM, with a spike almost as large as that of C. ANDERSONI, but its stem and leaf growth are not so vigorous as in the latter species; the bright yellow flowers are freely spotted with red, and usually produced in tall, branched spikes in the late Spring.


## DIACRIUM

The small genus of West Indian Orchids known as Diacrium is closely allied to Epidendrum, and sometimes placed under the latter. Only one species is at all commonly cultivated, and this is D. BICORNUTUM, which has thick pseudo-bulbs that are quite hollow. The fragrant flowers are borne eight or ten together in erect spikes, and they are white, the lip being dotted with purple, while the disk is yellow. The best way to manage DIACRIUM BICORNUTUM is to grow it in a teak basket in peat and sphagnum, and suspend it over a water-tank in the hottest house while it is growing freely, removing it to a lighter, drier position in a stove when resting. It is a charming Orchid when it flowers freely, and its flowers are very lasting and useful.

## EPI-CATTLEYA

There are a few hybrids of recent origin derived from crossing an Epidendrum with a Cattleya, but none are of outstanding horticultural merit. Some of the hybrids are very rare, and so do not appear before the public. Of those seen by the writer E.-c. MATUTINA (*E. radicans* x *C.Bowringiana*) is the best; it has carmine, yellow-lipped flowers, an inch and a half across, borne eight or ten together in a spike.

## EPI-LÆLIA

The Epi-lælias are not very prominently with us yet, and little is known of their real value or cultural needs, though probably the latter are easily provided in the Intermediate House. Eighteen or twenty hybrids have appeared, and the most conspicuous of these are—E.-L. CHARLESWORTHII (*E. radicans* x *L. cinnabarina*), E.-L. HARDYANA (*E. ciliare* x *L. anceps*), and E.-L. VEITCHII (*E. radicans* x *C. purpurata*). In all these the style of growth and flower most resembles the Epidendrum parent, but the flowers are larger and the growth dwarfer.

ONCIDIUM MACRANTHUM.

## ERIA

The genus Eria is mainly of botanical interest, and most of its members thrive best in the stove or Intermediate House. The flowers are small and seldom attractive. The species vary a good deal in habit, but are mostly low-growing and pseudo-bulbous. The inflorescence is generally a dense spike or raceme. Half a dozen of the most interesting species are E. ACERVATA, E. BARBATA, E. CONVALLARIOIDES, E. EXCAVATA, E. FLAVA, and E. STELLATA.

## ERIOPSIS

Although three species are known in gardens, only one of these comes before the public with any degree of regularity, and even it is somewhat rare. This is ERIOPSIS RUTIDOBULBON, which bears a long, drooping raceme of tawny orange flowers, shaded with purple. The temperature of the Intermediate House suits it, and though it must never be "dried off," it needs little water when resting. Fibrous peat will suffice for rooting medium.

## EULOPHIA

The Eulophias are widely distributed terrestrial Orchids, but they have few attractions for the majority of cultivators. Treated like Phaius, or grown in a bright, warm greenhouse, they are not without attractiveness, especially for those who like to grow plants not commonly found in gardens. Fibrous loam, leaf mould, and sand, form a suitable compost; when growing freely and flowering they need plenty of water, but very little will suffice when they are at rest, while at all times they like bright light.    The best species are E. GUINEENSIS, with large purple, green, and white flowers on a yard-high spike ; E. MACULATA, that has reddish-brown and white flowers ; and E. SAUNDERSIANA, which has green and purple-black flowers, and is a very striking plant.

## EULOPHIELLA

Two species are occasionally found in collections, and one of these, E. PEETERSIANA, is probably referable to Eulophia.    It is a strong grower, and has large yellowish flowers, carried many together on erect spikes, four feet high.    E. ELIZABETHÆ, from Madagascar, is a very pretty Orchid, but one that does not take kindly to cultivation.    Hundreds of plants were sold ten years or so ago, but very few of these remain alive, and of those that remain few ever flower satisfactorily.    This is unfortunate, as the horizontal or semi-drooping spikes, a foot long, carry several white flowers of great beauty ; each bloom is from two to three inches across, and its whiteness is enhanced by the yellow marks on the lip and by the deep, red-purple of the stems and the exterior of the sepals.    It appears to do best at the warmest end of the hottest stove, in a well-drained basket, grown in a mixture of peat, broken leaves, sphagnum, and sand.

## GONGORA

The Gongoras have a quaintness that is attractive, but the species are of little value except as curiosities.    They grow very much in the same way as Stanhopeas, and should be similarly

CATTLEYA PITTIANA.

treated, but it must be remembered that their flowers are not so large or fleshy as those of Stanhopeas. Three species may be selected for consideration, and these are—G. ATROPURPUREA, G. BUFONIA, and G. QUINQUINERVIS. In the first the flowers are purple-brown, and in the others yellow, with purple markings. In all cases the flowers are borne in pendulous racemes.

## GRAMMANGIS

One species, GRAMMANGIS ELLISII, from Madagascar, is in cultivation, but it is not often grown because it occupies considerable space, and does not flower freely. It has stout, squared pseudo-bulbs, and leaves that are often two feet long. The flowers are yellow, heavily marked with transverse lines of red-brown on the broad sepals ; the lip is white, streaked with red-purple. When it does flower, Grammangis Ellisii is a striking plant, as it may carry as many as thirty of its showy flowers on a long arching spike. It should be grown in the stove, in peat and sphagnum, and given an abundance of water at all times, except when at rest.

## GRAMMATOPHYLLUM

The difficulty attending the cultivation of Grammatophyllums is that they are large plants, and take up so much room that only in a few establishments can they be accommodated. Further, our Summers are not long and bright enough to ensure the specimens flowering with any degree of regularity. G. SPECIOSUM is the foremost species, and in all probability it is the largest growing Orchid, both in height and spread. There is a fine specimen in the Peradeniya Botanic Gardens, Ceylon, and a still larger one in the Botanic Gardens at Pinang, a plant of enormous size, dragged from its native swamps in the forest to the gardens by Mr C. Curtis when he was in charge, and planted in a conspicuous position in the beautiful gardens of that eastern island. At Kew there is a plant that fills a large space in the tank in the Victoria Lily House, where on several occasions it has produced spikes seven or eight feet long, carrying numbers of large yellow, purple-spotted flowers. Bright light, plenty of moisture, and peat, fibrous loam, and sphagnum to root in, with the highest temperature the plant houses afford, are the chief requirements of this wonderful Orchid. G. RUMPHIANUM (or *G. Fenzlianum*) is of smaller growth, and its flowers are yellow, heavily marked with bright red-brown. G. MEASURESIANUM seems to be but a slight variation of *G Rumphianum.*

## HABENARIA

Our wild Habenarias are very interesting, but the exotic species far excel them in size and beauty, and provide a small set of wonderful and attractive Orchids. The cultivated species come from widely distant lands; from the East Indies, from North America, from China, the Shan States, and from Madagascar. They are all terrestrial and deciduous, needing abundance of moisture when growing, but hardly any when resting. They have tuberous roots, and a little rosette of leaves, from the centre of which the flowering stem rises. There are four species that thoroughly deserve more extensive cultivation than they at present receive.

Well-drained pots or pans are the best receptacles, and a suitable compost consists of peat and sphagnum, with a few small pieces of old broken brick or limestone added. It is a good plan to place the

pot or pan in a slightly larger one when the plants die down and
go to rest, filling the space between the two pots with tightly
pressed sphagnum. The latter should be moistened occasionally,
and then the tubers in the inner pot will not become so dry as to
lose a large part of their vitality or even their life, while the danger
of causing the tubers to rot by the direct application of water to
the material in which they grow is obviated. Potting should be
done in the Spring, just as the new growth appears.

The following species are best grown in a stove temperature,
and raised near the glass; moderate shade is desirable all through
the season of active growth :—H. CARNEA is from the Langkawi
Islands, where it was found by the writer's namesake while on a
botanising expedition. It is a charming little species, about a foot
high when in flower; the broad leaves are deep green, freely
spotted with white, while the flowers are a lovely shade of flesh
pink, large for the size of the plant, the lip being over an inch
broad. This species was sent to Kew by its discoverer, and first
flowered in this country at Kew at the time the writer had charge
of the Orchid collection at that establishment. H. C. NIVOSA is a
beautiful pure white variety. H. PUSILLA is far better known as
*H. militaris*, but the former is the correct title. This is a low-
growing species from Cochin China, a foot or more in height when
in flower; it has narow, light-green leaves, and spikes of scarlet
flowers. H. RHODOCHEILA is very like *H. pusilla* in general
appearance, rather less in stature, of paler colour, but with a
vermilion lip. H. SUZANNÆ is now referred to PLATANTHERA
SUZANNÆ; it is the largest grower of the present selection, being
about two feet high, occasionally rising as high as three feet when
in full bloom. The flowers are large, white, fleshy, and the three-
lobed lip is finely and deeply fringed. H. SUZANNÆ ranks with
*Dendrobium Brymerianum* as a most wonderful floral development.

## HOULLETIA

A small genus of interesting Orchids, from Columbia and Brazil. The species will succeed in the stove if treated in the same way as advised for *Stanhopeas*. The leaves are large and erect, the racemes tall and erect, carrying from six to a dozen flowers. The sepals and petals are wide spread, mostly yellow or brown, with darker markings. The best species are H. BROCKLEHURSTIANA, H. CHRYSANTHA, and H. ODORATISSIMA.

## IONOPSIS

Two very pretty little Orchids belong to this genus, and they hail respectively from Brazil and Central America. They are of lowly growth, rarely exceeding five inches in height, but their branching panicles of small elegant flowers are eighteen inches long. I. PANICULATA has white, rosy-flushed flowers, with the lip stained at the base with purple. I. UTRICULARIOIDES is rather smaller than *I. paniculata*, and has white flowers with a rosy base to the lip. The Ionopsis grow best in the Intermediate House, in shallow pans or small baskets, planted in equal proportions of peat and sphagnum.

## IPSEA

The one species, ISPEA SPECIOSA, is not often cultivated, but it is a pretty and interesting plant from Ceylon, where it is found at a considerable elevation growing among the grass. It is deciduous, about eight inches high when in growth, and fifteen or eighteen inches high when in bloom. It has a tuberous root, and is best treated in the same way as the Pleiones or "Indian Crocuses," except that a stove temperature is at all times desirable. The fragrant flowers of IPSEA SPECIOSA are large for the size of the plant, orange-yellow, with reddish lines on the disk.

## MEGACLINIUM

The Megacliniums appear to be confined to Western and Eastern Tropical Africa. They are allied to the Bulbophyllums, and need to be grown in similar fashion. They are very quaint Orchids, but not a single species possesses high horticultural merit. The flowers are small, and borne along a flattened rhachis or spike, and in the case of M. BUFO these look like a row of tiny, green frogs sitting along the middle of the back of a small, flattened snake. Dr Lindley considered that all arguments against the transmigration of souls would have been superfluous had Pythagoras been familiar with M. BUFO. M. CLARKEI, M. FALCATUM, M. LEUCORHACHIS, M. MINUTUM, and M. TRISTE, are also interesting, though in no sense can they be regarded as beautiful.

## MICROSTYLIS

A genus of East Indian Orchids that need stove treatment and a long period of decided rest. Small pots or pans, and a compost of peat and sphagnum suits them, and an abundance of moisture when they are growing is essential. The species have interesting flowers, but they are not showy, and their greatest value lies in the beauty of their leaves, these being variously coloured with green, grey, purple, rose, red, cream and brown. M. CALOPHYLLA, M. CONGESTA, M. MACROCHILA, M. METALLICA, M. SCOTTII, and M. WALLICHII are the best species.

## MOOREA

The one known species of this Colombian genus, MOOREA IRRORATA, is represented in British gardens by very few specimens, and the plant is not offered in catalogues.   It grows about eighteen inches high, and bears tall spikes of fleshy, red-brown flowers, the yellow lip being marked with purple.   It is more remarkable for its rarity than its beauty.   The species first flowered at the Glas-nevin Botanic Gardens, Dublin, and bears the name of the clever Curator of that famous establishment, Mr F. W. Moore.

## MORMODES

The Mormodes have much in common with the Catasetums, and require similar cultural conditions, though they will succeed in a slightly lower temperature.   The most striking species are M. BADIUM, M. BUCCINATOR, M. LUXATA, M. OCANÆ, M. PARDINA, and M. ROLFEANA.

## NEOBENTHAMIA

This genus is at present represented by one species, N. GRACILIS, and it has slender, reed-like stems, five or six feet high, and pretty, white flowers in which the lip is white with purple spots and a central yellow band.   The plants require an abundance of water, a high temperature, and a compost of peat and sphagnum.

## ORNITHOCEPHALUS

ORNITHOCEPHALUS GRANDIFLORUS is occasionally met with in collections, but it has little to recommend it.   It grows about six

LÆLIA TENEBROSA, WALTON GRANGE VARIETY.

inches high, and has arching spikes of small, white and green flowers. The flowers are set closely together, and are each about three quarters of an inch across. It should be grown in pans, in peat, broken leaves, and sphagnum, and placed in a warm house.

## PAPHINIA

The Paphinias form a small family of interesting Orchids from South America. They need a shady place in the warmest house, and a continually moist atmosphere; but when not in full growth, a small quantity of water at the roots will suffice. They should be planted in peat, leaf mould, and sphagnum, in shallow, well-drained pans. The flowers are about four inches across, and rather short lived. The most notable species are P. CRISTATA, yellow, heavily marked with purple-brown, and with a curious tuft of hairs on the lip; and P. GRANDIFLORA, creamy white, marked with red-purple.

## PERISTERIA

The one species of horticultural merit in this genus is the old " Dove Orchid," a plant introduced long ago from Panama. It is PERISTERIA ELATA, a strong growing plant with broad, green leaves a yard high, and stiffly erect, stout spikes rising sometimes six feet high, and bearing on the upper portion a number of rounded, fleshy, white flowers, faintly speckled with purple. The winged column bears a fanciful resemblance to a Dove, hence the popular name, adapted from the native " Santos Spiritus," or " Holy Ghost Orchid." P. ELATA grows well in a shady part of an ordinary stove, and will make a large specimen if well treated. Abundance of water is necessary when new leaves or spikes are developing, and weak liquid manure may be given with advantage to a well-established specimen.    When the new leaves are completely developed, a season of rest, with little water given, is necessary; but as no dependence can be placed upon an annual crop of flowers, the species is not nearly so popular now that so many other and more easily accommodated Orchids are procurable.    Fibrous peat and loam, over ample drainage, make a suitable compost.

## PHAIO CALANTHE

In this family are grouped the hybrids derived from Phaius and Calanthe. It cannot be said that any of them are of very high horticultural merit, but they are interesting, and do not lack beauty. They approach most nearly to the Phaius, and need somewhat similar treatment. The principal hybrids are P.-c. ARNOLDIÆ (*Calanthe Regnieri* x *Phaius grandifolius*), P.-c. GRANDIS (*C. Darblayana* x *P. grandifolius*), P.-c. IRRORATA (*C. vestita* x *P grandifolius*), P. RUBY (*C. Ruby* x *P. Wallichii*), and P.-c. SEDENIANA (*C. Veitchii* x *P. grandifolius*).

## PHAIO CYMBIDIUM

Only one hybrid is at present recorded between Phaius and Cymbidium, and it is P.-c. CHARDWARENSE (*Cymbidium giganteum* x *Phaius Wallichii*).

## PLEUROTHALLIS

This is a very large genus, probably the largest, of Orchids, but while it contains many interesting species, and most of them are easily grown in the cool house, there are none of real horticultural merit, for even P. ROEZLII, a foot or more high, with fairly large, blackish flowers, is far more curious than beautiful. As a rule the flowers are quite small and inconspicuous, with green and dull purple colouring.

## RESTREPIA

The Restrepias are of lowly growth, akin to the Pleurothallis, and are easily grown in small pans or baskets in a cool house, in peat and sphagnum. They have small flowers, the joined lower sepals being the chief attraction. The best species are R. ANTENNIFERA, yellow and red; R. ELEGANS, yellow, with purple spots; R. MACULATA, yellow, with rows of red-brown spots; R. PANDURATA, whitish, with red - purple spots; R. STRIATA, yellow, with deep maroon stripes; and R. SANGUINEA, crimson.

## RHYNCHOSTYLIS

A small genus with one notable species, R. RETUSA, which is very like a Saccolabium, needs similar treatment, and is often known as *Saccolabium Blumei*. It has foot-long, pendulous, densely-flowered spikes of white flowers, spotted with deep violet-purple, and with a purple lip. R. R. HEATHII has pure white flowers, and R. R. MAJUS is larger than the type, and a very handsome Orchid.


## RODRIGUEZIA

The Rodriguezias, or Burlingtonias, to give them their old name, are dwarf plants, best grown in peat and sphagnum, in baskets suspended in the Intermediate House. They are evergreen, and therefore must always be kept moist at the roots. The flowers are pretty, borne in drooping spikes rather less than a foot long. The best are R. DECORA, with white flowers, sometimes pale rose, spotted with red, and a white lip; this has ascending rhizomes, and is best grown against a raft. R. FRAGRANS, white, with yellow throat, very fragrant; R. PUBESCENS, white and yellow; R. SECUNDA, rosy pink, with darker lip, one of the prettiest.


## SACCOLABIUM

The Saccolabiums are tropical epiphytal plants, chiefly from India, Burmah, and the Malay Peninsula. They have a Vanda-like habit, but are smaller, and range from a few inches up to a foot or so in height; they should be grown in the same way as the Aerides and Vandas, in a warm, moist atmosphere. The flowers are not large, but they are carried in rather dense, pendulous spikes that are produced from the axils of the leaves. The best are S. AMPULLACEUM, rosy carmine; S. BELLINUM, fleshy flowers, rather large for the family, yellow, spotted with purple, lip white and yellow, with purple spots; S. CURVIFOLIUM, a foot

STANHOPEA  T GR NA.

high, flowers orange-red; S. GIGANTEUM, more than a foot high, flowers white, spotted with purple, lip deep violet-purple; S. MINIATUM, small flowers, orange-red; S. VIOLACEUM, a foot or more high, flowers white with violet-purple spots, and violet-purple lip.

## SCHOMBURGKIA

The Schomburgkias are strong growers, and need the same treatment as Cattleyas. They do not flower with any degree of regularity, and therefore are not popular or valuable. The flowers are of moderate size, and carried, several together, in small spikes. S. LYONSII is white and purple, with yellow margin to the lip. S. TIBICINIS, the best known species, has purple-brown, undulate sepals and petals, and the lip is white, yellow and purple.

## SCUTICARIA

The two species of Scuticaria are remarkable for their long, pendulous, fleshy, terete leaves, and fleshy, short stemmed flowers, three inches across. They should be fixed to a block of wood and suspended in the stove, though S. HADWENII will do very well in an intermediate house. A little sphagnum about the roots is all that is needed as rooting material. Give plenty of water when growing and very little when resting. S. HADWENII is greenish yellow, with brown spots. S. STEELII is yellow, marked with deep red.

## SPATHOGLOTTIS

These are terrestrial, deciduous Orchids that may be grown in loam, peat, leaf-mould and sand, or in the usual peat and sphagnum mixture. They need a warm house, plenty of water when growth is vigorous, but only enough to keep the corm-like pseudo-bulbs plump during the time they are dormant. They are graceful plants, with long, plaited leaves, and spikes about eighteen inches or two feet high. The flowers are rounded, two or three inches across, bright yellow in S. AUREA and S. FORTUNEI, and rosy in S. VIEILLARDII. These are the three best species, but there are several hybrids that merit attention where Orchids of this kind are appreciated. These are S. COLMANII (*S. aurea* x *S. Veitchii*), S. KEWENSIS (*S. plicata* x *S. Vieillardii*), and S. VEITCHII (*S. aurea* x *S. Vieillardii*), often grown as *S. aureo-Vieillardii*.

## STANHOPEA

Stanhopeas have large flowers, and these are usually very attractive, but they are short lived, and cannot be used in floral decorations, hence they cannot be considered first-class. They are, however, worth growing for their interest and striking appearance, where room can be provided in a stove or intermediate house, near the roof glass. Basket culture is advised, and if crocks are used as drainage, these must be stood on edge and not laid flat, as the flower spikes are pendulous, and have a knack of pushing downwards through the compost and coming out at the bottom of the basket. New rooting material, peat and sphagnum, should be provided when new growth commences, and when growth has finished for the season, the plants should be placed in a bright position in a cooler house. S. EBURNEA, ivory white; S. INSIGNIS, yellow and purple; S. LOWII, yellow and white; S. TIGRINA (the best), red, yellow and white, very brilliant; and S. WARDII, golden yellow and purple, are the best to grow.

## TRICHOCENTRUM

T. ALBO-PURPUREUM and T. TIGRINUM are the most important members of this genus, and they are dwarf, with flowers about two inches across. The former is brown and white, and the latter greenish yellow, purple and white. The plants should be grown in a warm, moist house, in baskets hung near the roof glass.

## TRICHOPILIA

The Trichopilias come almost into the first-class division, as they are very attractive when in bloom, their flowers being of good size, pendulous, and produced freely from the base of the last pseudo-bulb. To grow them well and show them off to advantage, they should be placed in peat and sphagnum, in baskets, and suspended in an intermediate house, with the exception of T. SUAVIS, which will do well in the cool house. Careful watering is at all times necessary, as excess of moisture or sodden compost are fatal.

The best species are T. BACKHOUSEANA, white and yellow; T. COCCINEA, green, crimson and white; T. FRAGRANS, white and green; T. GALLEOTTIANA, yellow; T. SANGUINOLENTA, green, red-brown and white; and T. SUAVIS, large, fragrant flowers, white, freely spotted, and shaded with rose; there is a white variety of *T. suavis*—T. S. ALBA.

## TRICHOSMA

TRICHOSMA SUAVIS has slender stems, about six inches high, each bearing a pair of stout leaves, not quite so long as the stems. The flowers are an inch across, pure white, with yellow and crimson marks on the lip, fragrant and pretty. They are borne several together on a short spike springing up between the leaves. T. SUAVIS should be kept moist at all times, and grown in peat and sphagnum at the warm end of the cool house.

## VANILLA

The Vanillas are strong-growing, climbing Orchids, that thrive in a hot moist house. There are several species, with large, unattractive flowers and flat, deep-green leaves. They are interesting, however, especially V. PLANIFOLIA, which produces the Vanilla of commerce from the pods formed after the flowers have faded.

## WARSCEWICZELLA

A group of low-growing Orchids that are sometimes joined on to Zygopetalum. They are of tufted growth, with erect, green leaves, and medium-sized flowers carried on short stems near the base of the plant. The flowers are fleshy, and have a large lip. W. COCHLEARIS, W. DISCOLOR, W. LINDENI, W. WAILESIANA, and W. WENDLANDII are the principal species.

TR CHOP L A BACKHOUSEAN.\

# HARDY ORCHIDS

CONSIDERING the beauty of many of our native Orchids, it is surprising that lovers of hardy flowers do not take more kindly than they have done to the Hardy Orchids, as a class. One thing is quite certain, and it is that if those who have the opportunity would patiently cultivate a considerable number of the hardy species, both native and exotic, the success they would achieve would bring them much pleasure and credit, and their methods of culture would enable others to succeed. At present Hardy Orchids are not much cultivated; indeed, with the exception of Cypripedium spectabile, Orchis foliosa, O. latifolia and O. maculata, they are rarely found in gardens. Some of our native Orchids do well on the limestone, while others are found thriving in peaty bogs, but now that the Rock Garden and the Water Garden are recognised features in many establishments, it ought not to be difficult to find positions suitable for all the species that are worthy of cultivation.

Planting should be done as soon as the plants have died down in the Autumn, and the tuberous roots should not be exposed more than is absolutely necessary during the process. The half dozen Hardy Orchids described below are the best for a novice to commence with, and having obtained a fair measure of success with these, he or she may proceed with other gems such as CALYPSO BOREALIS, purple; CYPRIPEDIUM CALIFORNICUM, white; C. CANDIDUM, brown and white; C. GUTTATUM, white and rose-purple;

C. HUMILE (often grown as *C. acaule*), rosy purple; C. MACRAN THUM, rosy purple; C. PUBESCENS, yellow and brown; C. TIBETI CUM, red purple; EPIPACTIS PALUSTRIS, white and crimson; HABENARIA BIFOLIA and its variety CHLORANTHA, the Butterfly Orchis, white and greenish white; H. CILIARIS, yellow, finely fringed; OPHRYS APIFERA, the Bee Orchis, velvety-brown and yellow; O. MUSCIFERA, the Fly Orchis, green and purple; ORCHIS MASCULA, the Purple Orchis, purple; O. MILITARIS, the Soldier Orchis, lilac and red; SERAPIAS CORDIGERA, purple and crimson; and S. LINGUA, brown.

## THE BEST SPECIES

CYPRIPEDIUM CALCEOLUS.—A fine European plant, and one of the most beautiful of our native species; but now, alas, very rarely found wild. It grows well in loam and leaf mould, in a semi-shaded, fairly moist place, but does not need quite so much moisture as C. spectabile. About a foot, or rather more, in height, it flowers in the Summer, is sweetly scented, and has brownish purple sepals and petals, and a golden yellow lip.

CYPRIPEDIUM MONTANUM.—This North American species, sometimes known as *C. occidentale*, will thrive with *C. Calceolus*, and should be similarly treated. Its leafy stems grow about eighteen inches high, and are surmounted by two or three flowers, with brownish purple sepals and petals, and a white, red marked lip.

CYPRIPEDIUM SPECTABILE.—Unquestionably this is the finest of the hardy Lady's Slipper Orchids, and lovers of hardy flowers should spare no pains to cultivate it successfully. It has been largely exhibited during recent years, especially by Messrs Wm.

Cutbush & Son, Highgate, who have displayed splendid specimens in big pans at the Temple Show, in London, in May.

In the South-Western Counties and in Ireland this species grows and flowers beautifully, often rising two and a half feet high, and carrying a pair of its large, white, carmine-flushed flowers on each stem in the Summer. The lip is very much inflated, and often an inch and a half long. Semi-shade and a moist position suit this species, and, if a natural boggy position is not available, a bed of peat and leaf mould, with rough sandstone nodules added, will provide a good rooting medium, but it must be placed over a moist, but not stagnant, base. Put the tubers six inches deep and mulch with leaf mould in early Summer, as the tubers are more liable to suffer from heat than from cold. C. SPECTABILE (*C. Reginæ* is probably the correct name), is the Mocassin Flower of North America.

ORCHIS FOLIOSA.—No other hardy Orchid is such a success under cultivation as this Madeiran species. It needs a cool, shady position and plenty of moisture, and is found to do best in a compost of equal parts of fibrous loam and rough leaf mould. A bed of this material about a foot deep should be prepared for the reception of the tuberous roots, and October is certainly the best time for planting; deep planting will defeat the end in view, and if the crown of the tuber is about an inch below the surface of the soil after planting, that will be found quite deep enough. To secure fine spikes two to three feet high, and with about eight inches clothed with charming lilac-purple flowers in June and July, it is advisable to lift and replant this Orchid at the end of each second year, separating the newly-formed tubers and planting them at once. Probably no one grows this beautiful Orchid so well as Mr G. D. Davidson does, at Westwick, Norwich.

ORCHIS LATIFOLIA.—The Marsh Orchis attains a height of one and a half feet under favourable conditions, and produces its spikes of purple flowers in early Summer. It needs abundance of moisture, and consequently grows best in a peaty bog, or where there is a good depth of leaf mould. In other respects it needs similar treatment to O. foliosa.

O. MACULATA is one of the prettiest of our native Orchids, and thrives in fairly heavy garden soil. It varies in colour, but is usually lilac or pink, with deeper spots. The variety O. M. SUPERBA is exceptionally fine.

## *ADDENDA*

BRASSO-CATTLEYA (see p. 31); add B.-C. CLIFTONII (*B.-c. Veitchii* x *Cattleya Trianæ*).

CATTLEYA (see p. 44); add C. PITTIANA (*C. Dowiana* x *C. granulosa*); and C. ROBERTII (*C. Schilleriana* x *C. Schræderæ*), also known as *C. Robert de Wavrin.*

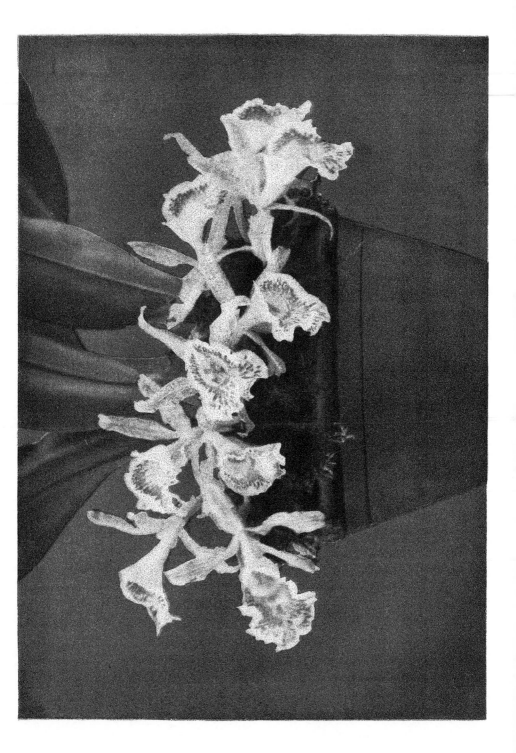

# A CALENDAR OF REMINDERS

## JANUARY

Clean the roof glass, inside and out, in all Orchid houses.

If lath roller-blinds are fixed to the houses, let these down at night, to afford protection and reduce the need for hard firing.

Thoroughly sponge and clean the plants, especially those that will soon start into new growth.

Sow ripe Orchid seeds early in the month.

Secure stocks of imported Dendrobiums as early as possible.

Get together a good supply of clean pots and crocks.

Prepare and store peat, loam, last year's Oak and Beech leaves, and sphagnum.

Sterilise the Oak and Beech leaves by enclosing them in a canvas bag, and placing them in boiling water for ten minutes. Afterwards dry the leaves before use.

See that all labels are sound and the writing legible.

Secure a supply of Bracken rhizomes, cut these into short lengths, and sterilise by immersion in boiling water.

Hunt for slugs at night, and set traps of grain and cabbage leaves for them.

See that the water in the tank is one or two degrees warmer

than the temperature of the house before it is used for watering. After rain and snow the temperature of the water falls quickly.

After Calanthes have finished flowering, allow them to become quite dry, and store them on a shelf in a light position.

The temperature of the Odontoglossum House should not fall below 50 degrees at night.   Blinds and mats will help to keep the house warm, and their use is better than excessive fire heat.


## FEBRUARY

Winter-flowering Cypripediums now out of flower should be potted as necessary, and large plants should be now divided if increase of stock is desired.

Vandas, Aerides, and kindred Orchids should be potted or top-dressed with new sphagnum.

*Oncidium Marshallianum* is often imported at this season; secure a few plants, and clean and pot them at once.

Sow seeds of Cattleyas, Lælias, Lælio-cattleyas, and other epiphytal Orchids.

The terrestrial Phaius, now throwing up their flower spikes, should be encouraged by increased warmth and a little weak liquid cow manure.

Where canvas blinds only are used for shading, and these have been stored in a dry place for the Winter, examine them, make good any defects, and place in position again ready for use.

CATTLEYA C TR NA.

## MARCH

Increase the amount of moisture in Orchid houses by damping floors and stages frequently; the atmosphere outside is usually dry this month, and bright sunshine generally accompanies a low temperature and dry winds.

Shading must be given during the brightest hours of the day, as the plants cannot stand as much sunshine at the end of the Winter as at the end of the Summer.

Deciduous Dendrobiums should be potted and top-dressed as soon as they pass out of flower, and encouraged to grow vigorously.

Seedling Orchids that are sufficiently large should be potted off separately.

Thunias will commence new growth towards the end of the month, and potting must not be delayed.

Odontoglossums that were not potted in the Autumn may need that attention now, and it is a mistake to defer the operation until warm weather arrives.

Calanthes must be potted as soon as their new growth advances.

Let Mexican Lælias have the benefit of all light and sunshine, and only give them sufficient water to keep the pseudo-bulbs and leaves plump.

Evergreen Dendrobiums will need additional moisture to assist them in the development of their flower spikes.

Pot *Miltonia Roezlii* if the plants need new rooting material.

o

*Miltonia vexillaria* should be potted annually, and where this operation was not carried out in the Autumn potting should be done at once, for although new roots and flower spikes appear simultaneously, no harm will come to the latter if potting is carefully done early in the month.

## APRIL

Many Orchids will be in a condition to need and appreciate new rooting material now. Calanthes not yet potted, late flowering Dendrobiums, Catasetums, Chysis, Cycnoches, and Lycastes that have finished flowering will all need attention.

Damp down the floors and stages early in the day, as soon as the temperature rises by natural heat.

Pay great care to shading, and ventilate with equal care. Admit air chiefly by means of the lower ventilators; top ventilation tends to dry the atmosphere quickly and severely. Leave the lower ventilators on the lee side of the cool houses open a little all night.

Odontoglossums not in flower may be sprayed very lightly overhead in the morning on all bright days.

Sphagnum will grow freely at this season, and care must be taken to prevent it from overgrowing seedlings, or endangering the new growths of older Orchids. Clip off excessive sphagnum growth with sharp scissors.

## MAY

Ventilate early in the day, and close the houses early in the afternoon. Open the lower ventilators of cool houses a little

ODONTOGLOSSUM URO-SKINNERI.

towards evening.  Almost all Orchids will need abundance of atmospheric moisture at this season.

*Vanda teres* will need potting as soon as its flowers have faded.

Pot Anguloas as they pass out of bloom.

Shade Odontoglossums early in the day, and if the houses face south or east, it may be desirable to thinly coat the roof glass with a permanent shading of whitening and milk, or other suitable preparation, as this will obviate the need of lowering the blinds so very early, and allow them to be drawn up earlier in the afternoon than would be otherwise possible.

As Summer-flowering Cypripediums pass out of flower they should be potted as necessary.

*Miltonia vexillaria* flowers this month, and before the blooms expand the plants should be very carefully cleaned, so that thrips or other insects do not damage the flowers.

*Lycaste Skinnerii* flowers over a long period, and as the flowers fade the plants should have prompt attention, and be potted if they need it.

*Cattleya Warscewiczii* must be watered sparingly at this season of the year, and given a light position.

Pot or top-dress Mexican Lælias as soon as they begin to make new growths and roots.

*Epiphronitis Veitchii* is best potted and propagated at this season, as soon as it has finished flowering.

## JUNE

Insect pests increase rapidly in the Summer; therefore special care is needed to keep the plants clean.  Vaporise or fumigate the houses at fortnightly intervals, and dip all plants that are infested in an approved insecticide.

Autumn-flowering Cattleyas and Lælias will develop and ripen their growths better in good light than under heavy shade. Shade lightly during the middle of the day

Secure and pot up imported Cattleyas and Lælias.

Afford deciduous Dendrobiums plenty of heat, and syringe them freely.

*Miltonia vexillaria* needs little water at the roots from the time it passes out of flower until the Autumn. The cool house is the best place for the plants until September.

All Orchids growing freely, and also the cool Odontoglossums, will benefit by a daily spraying overhead. Clear soft water only should be used, and it is better applied through a sprayer than a syringe, unless the latter is used by a skilful and experienced person.

Many of the Phaius will need potting as soon as they have finished flowering.


## JULY

Seedlings raised from seeds sown early in the new year will in many cases be large enough to be pricked out into store pots, or even to be placed singly in tiny pots.

Pot cool Oncidiums that need such attention.

The need of cleanliness in Orchid culture cannot be too strongly emphasised. Amateurs with small experience often pay too much attention to the cleanliness of pots and pans and floors, and far too little at this season of the year to the cleanliness of the plants themselves.

Where a gravel or flagged path runs past the cool houses it should be hosed or otherwise damped down in the evening, as this creates a pleasantly moist atmosphere, which, passing through the lower ventilators, benefits Odontoglossums, etc.

*Miltonia vexillaria* should no longer remain in the intermediate house, but be given a place in the cool house until growth begins again in the Autumn.

Importations of Odontoglossums frequently arrive at this season of the year, and a few plants purchased annually give added interest to the collection.

Any Cattleyas that are sending out new roots and are not coming into flower should be potted.

Many of the Cymbidiums will require more root-room or new rooting material.

## AUGUST

Calanthes will be growing freely, and need abundance of water. A little weak liquid cow manure, given once or twice a week to healthy, vigorous plants, will result in strong flower spikes later on.

Stanhopeas and allied Orchids usually make new growth soon after or while flowering, and should receive prompt attention.

Towards the end of the month the potting of cool Odontoglossums should be taken in hand, so that the plants may receive the benefit of pleasant Autumn weather, and become established again before Winter.

At the end of August all shading painted on to the roof glass should be washed off.

*Cattleya Warscewiczii* is generally in a condition to benefit by potting as soon as its flowers have faded.

The heating apparatus will not be required much during July and August, therefore full advantage should be taken of the warm weather to examine boilers and pipes, make good any defects, or provide new parts, so that all may be in perfect order before cold weather begins.

## SEPTEMBER

All cool Odontoglossums that need such attention should be potted as early as possible this month. There is no doubt that August and September afford the best possible time for this operation.

Mexican Lælias should receive all the light obtainable, except bright mid-day sunshine, and be syringed lightly on fine days. Close the house early in the afternoon, so as to encourage growth.

Vandas and similar Orchids will need much less shading now; the aim should be to ripen up the growths and leaves, so that they may the better stand the dull days of Winter.

Encourage Winter-flowering Cypripediums by allowing them increased light, sufficient root moisture, and an occasional watering with clear soot-water.

Cool Masdevallias should be potted early in the month.

Deciduous Dendrobiums will in many cases have finished their growth, and need cooler and drier conditions, and a light, sunny position.

LÆLIO-CATTLEYA LUSTRE.

Spathoglottis begin to make new growth at this time of year, and will need to be re-potted.

Even where no shading has been painted on the roof, there will be an accumulation of dust, therefore the outside of the glass should be washed.

## OCTOBER

Very little shading will be needed from now until the early Spring. On very bright days the blinds may be let down for an hour or two, but, provided the leaves do not suffer, full advantage of all available light should be taken so that leaves and pseudo bulbs may be rendered firm and able to pass safely through the Winter.

Odontoglossums will be growing, therefore shading must still be provided for them in bright weather.

Vandas will need a fair supply of water until the pale green tips of the new roots are sealed over; the supply must be then greatly reduced until new growth commences next year.

Calanthes will be losing their leaves, and consequently need less water at the roots, but they must not become dry, or the advancing flower spikes will suffer. Afford them a light position, and give support to the spikes as soon as this is necessary.

Remove *Miltonia vexillaria* from the cool house to the intermediate house early in the month or at the end of September.

Where ripe Odontoglossum seeds have been secured by hybridisation, sow a portion now and keep the rest until January.

## NOVEMBER

Keep the roof glass clean.  In smoky districts and in towns the roof glass should be washed down once a week during November, December, and January.  See that the roof is water-tight before commencing the work, and apply the water so that it is not forced upward under the laps of the glass.

Scarcely any potting is necessary in November, and the principal work among Orchids will consist in managing the heating apparatus, and cleaning the plants and houses.

Put slender stakes to the flowers of Cypripediums, and afford neat ties.

Keep a sharp lookout for slugs, tiny snails, cockroaches, and other pests.

*Cælogyne cristata*, *Dendrobium nobile*, *D. aureum*, and *D. Wardianum* may be placed in a warmer house if flowers are needed for Christmas and the new year.  Only a few plants should be so treated, and these the most advanced.

Some late-flowering Cattleyas may need to be potted, such as *C. labiata*, *C. Dowiana*, *C. Hardyana*, etc., and if they are making new roots they must not be neglected in this respect.

## DECEMBER

When the flowers of Winter-flowering Cypripediums have fully developed, they should not be allowed to remain on the plants until they fade, as this imposes a severe strain.  They will last a long time in good condition if cut and placed in water.

*Cattleya Warscewczii* will be finishing its growth and need a smaller supply of moisture.

Winter-flowering Cypripediums may be potted after they have flowered, but it is better to wait until the new year.

Keep the roof glass clean.   Use the lath roller blinds at night as a means of protection from frost; the use of blinds economises fuel.

Thoroughly clean the inside of all houses.   Make good any defects in the staging.

# INDEX

# INDEX

# INDEX

231

9 781330 484906